. . . a teacher's guide to accompany

Write ONE

WRITE SOURCE®

GREAT SOURCE EDUCATION GROUP
a Houghton Mifflin Company
Wilmington, Massachusetts

Write ONE
About the Teacher's Guide

It's important for you to know a few things about your *Write One Teacher's Guide* before you begin to use it.

Previewing ● The opening section provides a quick tour of the handbook to help you become familiar with its basic features. The next section—"Getting Started Activities"—contains guidelines and reproducible activity sheets that you can use to introduce the handbook to your students.

Planning ● The section "Using *Write One* in the Classroom" provides a variety of ideas for planning instruction. The next three sections contain summaries of all the handbook chapters related to writing and learning skills. Finally, the "Handbook Minilessons" section offers a variety of short activities to use along with the handbook. (At least one minilesson is provided for each handbook chapter.)

Managing ● "Evaluating/Assessing/Monitoring" offers suggestions for evaluating writing and addressing basic grammar and punctuation skills. Also included in this section is valuable information related to peer conferencing and portfolio assessment.

Supplementing ● The final sections in the *Teacher's Guide* serve as a resource for enhancing instruction with the handbook. "Reading-Writing Connection" lists high-interest trade books that are related to major chapters in the handbook and can be helpful in planning units. The "Resources for Teachers" section lists additional resources that may help during planning. Finally, "Program Overview" highlights the coordinating program for grade one.

Authors: Dave Kemper and Carol Elsholz

Printed in the United States of America

International Standard Book Number: 0-669-45978-X

3 4 5 6 7 8 9 10 -DBH- 02 01 00 99

What You'll Find Inside

A QUICK Tour

Write One Student Handbook

    Write One serves as a language arts handbook for grade one. It will help your students improve their abilities **to write** and **to learn** (in the classroom, in small groups, and independently). This quick tour will highlight the major points of interest in each section of the handbook.

1 The Process of Writing

Students will use this section of the handbook to become acquainted with the writing process.

Jenny Writes

It's writing time in Room 101. Luke is planning a story. Rosa is writing a poem. And Ben is writing something silly.

10

Colorful illustrations and a personal tone are used throughout *Write One*.

Steps in the Writing Process

The **writing process** has five steps: planning, writing, revising, checking, and publishing.

I

PLAN
- Talk.
- Draw.
- Think.
- Write lists.

Things Pets Need
1. food
2. water
3. love
4. a plas to sleep
5. toys

22

Using Capital Letters

You use **capital letters** in your writing.

The **first word** in a sentence

Bears catch fish.

Names

Sandy   Trout Lake

The word **I**

When can I go fishing?

30

2 The Forms of Writing

When students are ready to make an alphabet book, write a poem, or start a personal journal, this is the section to turn to.

Write One addresses many forms of writing, from friendly notes to reports.

Making Alphabet Books

Making an **alphabet book** is as easy as ABC. You can make one by yourself or with your class.

- Choose a topic.
- List words about the topic for the letters of the alphabet.

Words About Our School

A art   G gym
B bus   H heart
C calendar   I ice cream
D dancing   J jokes
E Eastview   K kindness
F friends   L lunch

Writing Poems

Writing poems is like making little word pictures. Think of the best words to use in your poems.

Couplet
- Write **two** lines that rhyme.

> Sometimes comets in space
> Look like they're having a race.
> – Max

Triplet
- Write **three** lines that rhyme.

> Colors, colors everywhere,
> Colors here and colors there,
> Colors on the shirt I wear.
> – Shiere

74

Writing in Journals

A **journal** is your very own place for writing. You can write in your journal every day.

- Write the date.
- Draw a picture if you want to.
- Write about things you do and think about.

October 7

I ride my bike fast.
I can make it jump.
I ride with my dad.

38

3 Reading and Word Study

For enhancing your students' reading skills, have them turn to "Reading and Word Study."

Reading to Understand

Reading takes lots of thinking. You should think before, during, and after reading.

Think Before Reading

LOOK over your reading.
- Check the title.
- Look at the pictures.

PREDICT what will be in the reading.

82

Aa

alligator

bat
map
Sam

ape

cake
play
rain

Write One contains lots of easy-to-use pages for young readers and writers.

Tt

turtle

table
teacher
television
today
tooth
toy
turkey

115

Word-study skills are clearly demonstrated.

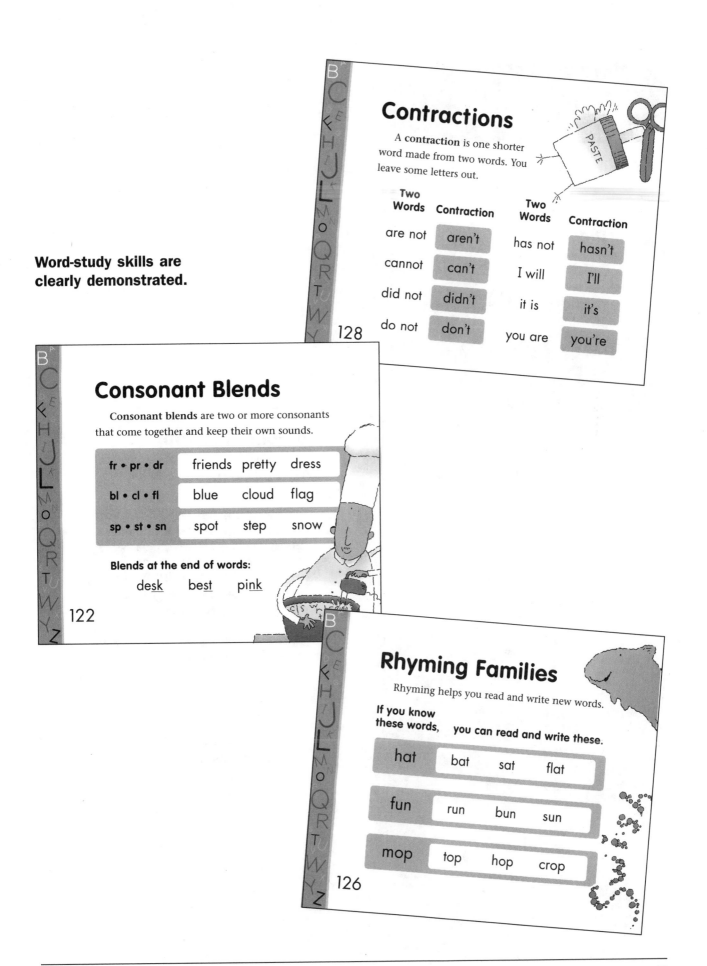

Contractions

A **contraction** is one shorter word made from two words. You leave some letters out.

Two Words	Contraction	Two Words	Contraction
are not	aren't	has not	hasn't
cannot	can't	I will	I'll
did not	didn't	it is	it's
do not	don't	you are	you're

128

Consonant Blends

Consonant blends are two or more consonants that come together and keep their own sounds.

fr • pr • dr	friends	pretty	dress
bl • cl • fl	blue	cloud	flag
sp • st • sn	spot	step	snow

Blends at the end of words:

de<u>sk</u>   be<u>st</u>   pi<u>nk</u>

122

Rhyming Families

Rhyming helps you read and write new words.

If you know these words, **you can read and write these.**

hat	bat	sat	flat
fun	run	bun	sun
mop	top	hop	crop

126

4 The Student Almanac

Theme words, math charts, full-color maps—*Write One* has all kinds of information for young learners.

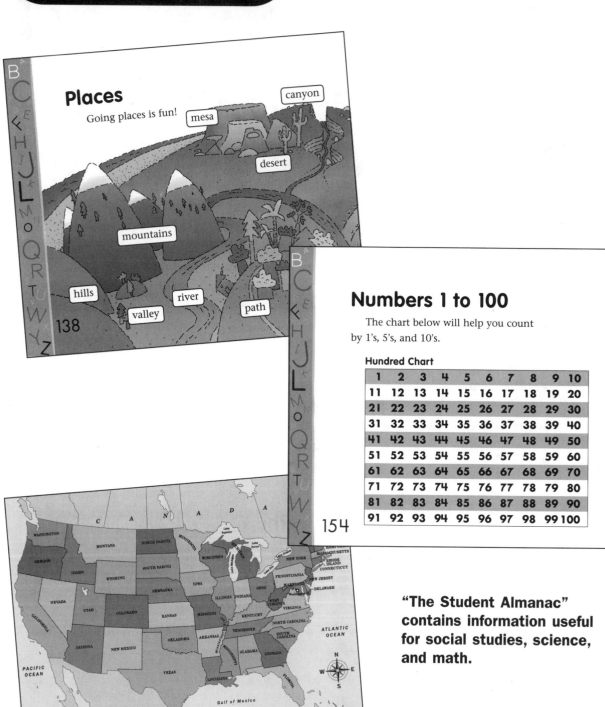

Places

Going places is fun!

canyon

mesa

desert

mountains

hills

river

valley

path

138

Numbers 1 to 100

The chart below will help you count by 1's, 5's, and 10's.

Hundred Chart

1	2	3	4	5	6	7	8	9	10
11	12	13	14	15	16	17	18	19	20
21	22	23	24	25	26	27	28	29	30
31	32	33	34	35	36	37	38	39	40
41	42	43	44	45	46	47	48	49	50
51	52	53	54	55	56	57	58	59	60
61	62	63	64	65	66	67	68	69	70
71	72	73	74	75	76	77	78	79	80
81	82	83	84	85	86	87	88	89	90
91	92	93	94	95	96	97	98	99	100

154

United States

⊕ National Capital
- - - State Boundaries

149

"The Student Almanac" contains information useful for social studies, science, and math.

Getting Started ACTIVITIES

Write One was developed by experienced teachers and writers for students in first grade and beyond. More than anything else, we wanted to put together a handbook that students would find very helpful and very enjoyable to use. Over the past several years, teachers have told us what they like best about our other handbooks, and what they do when the book is first put into the hands of their students.

Learning About the Handbook

Many of their suggestions, plus some of our own, are contained in this section of your *Teacher's Guide*. Of special interest to you will be the suggested sequences of activities on pages 9-10 for introducing the handbook to your students, the reproducible activity sheets on pages 11-15, and the start-up minilessons on pages 16-19.

About the **Write One**
Handbook

Write One serves as a writing and learning resource for students in grade one. Here are four important ways that the handbook can be used.

1. Core Program Resource

Students use the handbook to help them complete the activities in the *Write One Language Series* program. (The handbook and coordinating program can serve as the foundation for an exciting research-based language arts curriculum.)

2. Writing-Reading Connection

Students use the handbook as a resource of ideas and words for their writing and reading activities.

3. All-School Handbook

Students get an early introduction to using a handbook as a resource for finding information related to language arts, social studies, science, and math.

4. Study Helper

When students are writing or studying at home, *Write One* will help them with their work. Young learners (and their parents) will especially appreciate all of the handy word lists, guidelines, and models in the handbook.

Start-Up Ideas

The start-up activities in this teacher's guide help you introduce your students to the *Write One* handbook. These ideas include scavenger hunt blackline masters and minilessons.

▶ **Scavenger hunts** show students the variety of information contained in their handbooks.

▶ **Minilessons** offer brief lessons from all four sections of the handbook.

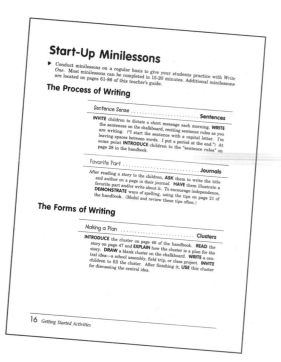

Start-Up Minilessons

▶ Conduct minilessons on a regular basis to give your students practice with *Write One*. Most minilessons can be completed in 15-20 minutes. Additional minilessons are located on pages 61-86 of this teacher's guide.

The Process of Writing

Sentence Sense .... **Sentences**

INVITE children to dictate a short message each morning. **WRITE** the sentences on the chalkboard, reciting sentence rules as you are writing. ("I start the sentence with a capital letter. I'm leaving spaces between words. I put a period at the end.") At some point **INTRODUCE** children to the "sentence rules" on page 28 in the handbook.

Favorite Part .... **Journals**

After reading a story to the children, **ASK** them to write the title and author on a page in their journal. **HAVE** them illustrate a favorite part and/or write about it. To encourage independence, **DEMONSTRATE** ways of spelling, using the tips on page 21 of the handbook. (Model and review these often.)

The Forms of Writing

Making a Plan .... **Clusters**

INTRODUCE the cluster on page 46 of the handbook. **READ** the story on page 47 and **EXPLAIN** how the cluster is a plan for the story. **DRAW** a blank cluster on the chalkboard. **WRITE** a central idea—a school assembly, field trip, or class project. **INVITE** children to fill the cluster. After finishing it, **USE** this cluster for discussing the central idea.

To begin, you may want to simply invite students to look through *Write One* for pages or pictures that they especially like. Let them share their discoveries with the class. Then read and discuss "Jenny Writes" on pages 10-19 in the handbook.

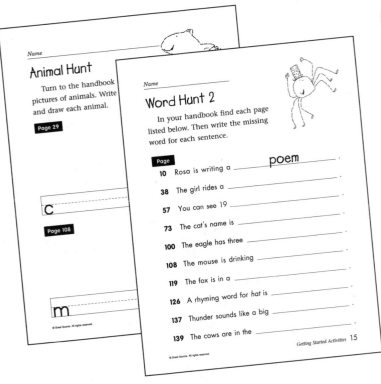

Name

Animal Hunt

Turn to the handbook pictures of animals. Write and draw each animal.

Page 29

c

Page 108

m

© Great Source. All rights reserved.

Name

Word Hunt 2

In your handbook find each page listed below. Then write the missing word for each sentence.

Page

10 Rosa is writing a _____ poem

38 The girl rides a _____

57 You can see 19 _____

73 The cat's name is _____

100 The eagle has three _____

108 The mouse is drinking _____

119 The fox is in a _____

126 A rhyming word for *hat* is _____

137 Thunder sounds like a big _____

139 The cows are in the _____

Getting Started Activities 15

© Great Source. All rights reserved.

▶ The five scavenger hunts will take children to many places in the handbook. Use these as guided activities.

Another way to introduce your students to *Write One* is to point out the four color-coded sections of the handbook.

▶ Introduce "The Process of Writing" (the **GREEN** section). Read "Jenny Writes" together. Encourage children to share how they perceive themselves as writers. Talk about Jenny, Luke, Rosa, and Ben as writers. Assign the scavenger hunt blackline master "Writing Buddies" as an independent or guided activity.

▶ Introduce "The Forms of Writing" (the **RED** section). Tell children about the many different forms of writing. Focus on forms that are familiar, such as "Writing Friendly Notes" (pages 42-43), and "Writing Poems" (pages 74-77). Be sure to share some of the writing models with the children.

▶ Introduce "Reading and Word Study" (the **YELLOW** section). Help students find the alphabet pages beginning on page 96. Explore these pages for letters, sounds, and words they know. Assign the scavenger hunt "Letter Search" or turn to the list of high-frequency words, "Using Everyday Words" (pages 86-89), and have students work on the scavenger hunt "Word Hunt 1."

▶ Introduce "The Student Almanac" (the **BLUE** section). Give children time to discover the variety of information available here. Then use any of the related minilessons found on pages 79-86 of this teacher's guide.

Use these start-up ideas to best meet the needs of your students.

Writing Buddies

Write the names of the children from the story "Jenny Writes," pages 10-19 in the handbook.

Draw your picture.
Write your name, too.

Letter Search

Search for these letters in the yellow section of your handbook. Begin on page 96. Color the letters to match the color of the letters in the handbook.

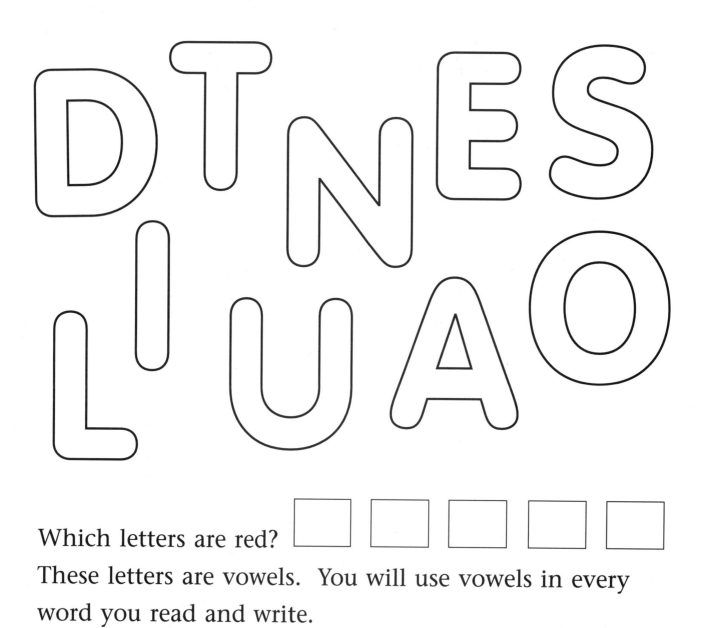

Which letters are red? ☐ ☐ ☐ ☐ ☐

These letters are vowels. You will use vowels in every word you read and write.

Name

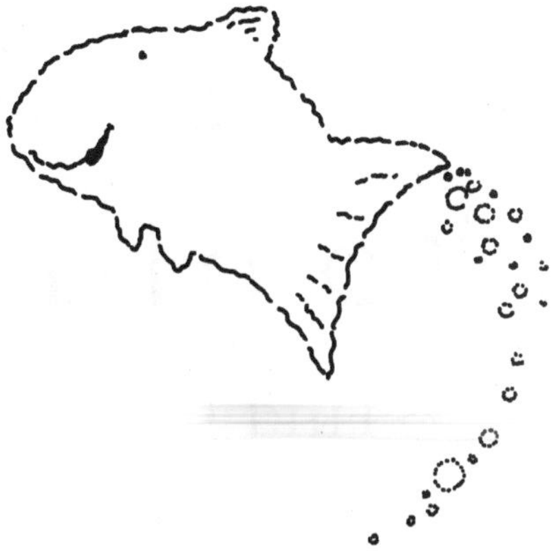

Animal Hunt

Turn to the handbook pages to find pictures of animals. Write each name and draw each animal.

Page 29

c

Page 43

l

Page 108

m

Pages 126-127

f

Word Hunt 1

Find the word lists beginning on
page 86. Write one word for each letter.

A ____and____   M _____

B _____   O _____

D _____   R _____

F _____   S _____

H _____   T _____

I _____   W _____

L _____   Y _____

Word Hunt 2

In your handbook find each page listed below. Then write the missing word for each sentence.

Page

10   Rosa is writing a _____ poem _____ .

38   The girl rides a _____ .

57   You can see 19 _____ .

73   The cat's name is _____ .

100   The eagle has three _____ .

108   The mouse is drinking _____ .

119   The fox is in a _____ .

126   A rhyming word for *hat* is _____ .

137   Thunder sounds like a big _____ .

139   The cows are in the _____ .

Start-Up Minilessons

▶ Conduct minilessons on a regular basis to give your students practice with *Write One*. Most minilessons can be completed in 15-20 minutes. Additional minilessons are located on pages 61-86 of this teacher's guide.

The Process of Writing

Sentence Sense . . . . **Sentences**

INVITE children to dictate a short message each morning. **WRITE** the sentences on the chalkboard, reciting sentence rules as you are writing. ("I start the sentence with a capital letter. I'm leaving spaces between words. I put a period at the end.") At some point **INTRODUCE** children to the "sentence rules" on page 28 in the handbook.

Favorite Part . . . . **Journals**

After reading a story to the children, **ASK** them to write the title and author on a page in their journal. **HAVE** them illustrate a favorite part and/or write about it. To encourage independence, **DEMONSTRATE** ways of spelling, using the tips on page 21 of the handbook. (Model and review these tips often.)

The Forms of Writing

Making a Plan . . . . **Clusters**

INTRODUCE the cluster on page 46 of the handbook. **READ** the story on page 47 and **EXPLAIN** how the cluster is a plan for the story. **DRAW** a blank cluster on the chalkboard. **WRITE** a central idea—a school assembly, field trip, or class project. **INVITE** children to fill the cluster. After finishing it, **USE** this cluster for discussing the central idea.

Reading and Word Study

Hunt and List .... **Consonants**

DIVIDE the class into teams of four to six children. **GIVE** each team a consonant and a long strip of paper. **INVITE** them to hunt for and list all the words they can find that begin with that letter. (You may ask them to search *Write One* or let them explore the classroom.) After 10 to 15 minutes of hunting and listing, **MEET** to make a class list.

Sort and Re-sort .... **Everyday Words**

TAPE a strip of paper (about 6" × 36") on the chalkboard. **LIST** 10 words from "Everyday Words," handbook pages 86-89. Then **CUT** and **SORT** the words according to categories (length, rhyme, initial sounds, etc.). **RE-SORT** the words according to new categories. **GIVE** students smaller strips of paper and let them write 10 words, cutting and sorting as you have modeled. (This activity can be an individual or a small-group activity.)

Sun Fun .... **Rhyming**

READ some of the rhyming words on pages 126-127. **WRITE** *fish, fun, mop,* and *hat* on a chalkboard or chart paper. Together, **GENERATE** more rhyming words for each word. Have fun creating two-word rhymes from the lists (sun fun, mop top, etc.). These little twosomes are fun to illustrate.

What's missing? .... **Rhyming**

COPY a favorite rhymed poem onto the chalkboard or chart paper. **COVER** one of a pair of rhyming words. **READ** through the poem, asking the children to supply the missing words. **LIST** the rhyming pairs and point out spelling patterns. **ASK** children for more words that rhyme, and add these to the lists.

The Student Almanac

I choose green. . . . . **Colors**

INTRODUCE children to the color words on pages 134-135 in the handbook. **ASK** a volunteer to choose a favorite color and share a sentence about it. On an overhead or the chalkboard, **WRITE** the sentence. **CONTINUE** the activity using other colors. **FINISH** by playing "I Spy" for colors in the classroom.

Off we go! . . . . **Places**

MAKE a class chart (see below) of places to go in vehicles. **USE** handbook pages 138-139 for this activity. **FILL** in the chart with the students' suggestions. You may want to **INCLUDE** places that aren't named in the handbook.

boat	car	tractor	jet
ocean			

Before, After, Between . . . . **Numbers**

Look at the handbook pages 134-135. **HELP** students discover how the fruit, words, and numbers on the trees are related. **INTRODUCE** a guessing game for small groups. One person says, "I'm thinking of a number that comes before, or after, another number." Or, "I'm thinking of a number that comes between this number and that number." Another person guesses the number. (At another time consider creating a class mural of trees, fruit, numbers, and number words.)

Weather Report . . . . **Weather Words**

INTRODUCE the words and weather symbols on page 137 of the handbook. **ENCOURAGE** the children to figure out the words by looking at the symbols. **REMIND** them that picture clues are very helpful for learning new words. **INVITE** the children to choose a word and share what they like to do in that kind of weather. Then **HAVE** them draw pictures and label them with appropriate weather words.

Yummy! . . . . **Food Pyramid**

INVITE the children to draw four of their favorite foods. **HELP** them label the foods. With their pictures in front of them, **INTRODUCE** the food pyramid (pages 142-143 of the handbook) and explain what it means. **ASK** the children to find their foods on the pyramid. **FIND OUT** how students feel about their choices after finding them on the pyramid.

Discoveries . . . . **Five Senses**

READ and **DISCUSS** the poem and picture about the senses on handbook pages 146-147. Then, on a chalkboard or an overhead, **COMPLETE** the sentences below. **ASK** students for several suggestions for each one.

Bees sound _____ .
Ice cream tastes _____ .
Books look _____ .
Beach balls feel _____ .
Flowers smell _____ .

Ice Cream . . . . **Bar Graphs**

LIST children's favorite ice-cream flavors. **FIND** the four favorites. Using handbook page 156 as a model, **CREATE** a bar graph with colored scoops of ice cream. (You may want to create a fifth category called "Other.") **USE** handbook page 156 as a model for the framework and details of the bar graph.

Answer Key

Writing Buddies (page 11)

Luke	**Jenny**
Rosa	**Ben**

Letter Search (page 12)

I   U   A   E   O

Animal Hunt (page 13)

p. 29 **cat**

p. 43 **ladybug**

p. 108 **mouse**

pp. 126-127 **fish**

Word Hunt (page 14)

Answers will vary.

Word Hunt 2 (page 15)

p. 10   **poem**

p. 38   **bike**

p. 57   **butterflies**

p. 73   **Pumpkin**

p. 100   **eggs**

p. 108   **milk**

p. 119   **box**

p. 126   **bat**, **sat**, or **flat**

p. 137   **BOOM**

p. 139   **meadow**

Using *Write One* in the CLASSROOM

Teachers often ask how *Write One* can be used in their classrooms. The answer to that question is easy. Teachers should think of *Write One* as their teacher's aide, on hand to help students at all times—during class, throughout the school day, and later at home—with their writing, reading, and learning. The following pages provide ideas for making the handbook work in the classroom.

Framework of WRITING ACTIVITIES

The types of writing in *Write One* are listed below in a possible framework or sequence of activities, moving from personal writing to writing that is more inventive and reflective. Teachers can use this framework as a starting point when planning a writing program with the handbook.

PERSONAL WRITING

Recording	**Writing in Journals (p. 38)**
Recalling and Remembering	**Writing Stories About Me (p. 46)**

SUBJECT WRITING

Introducing	**Writing About Others (p. 50)**
Describing	**Writing a Description (p. 52)** **Writing Captions (p. 56)**
Reporting	**Writing in Learning Logs (p. 68)**
Corresponding	**Writing Friendly Notes (p. 42)** **Writing Friendly Letters (p. 44)**
Informing	**Writing Directions (p. 54)**
Searching and Researching	**Writing Reports (p. 62)** **Making Alphabet Books (p. 66)**

CREATIVE WRITING

Imagining	**Writing Stories (p. 72)**
Inventing	**Writing Lists (p. 40)** **Writing Poems (p. 74)** **Writing with Patterns (p. 78)**

REFLECTIVE WRITING

Reviewing	**Writing About Books (p. 58)**

HB—*Write One* Student Handbook
PG—*Language Series Program Guide* (Ring Binder)

Week   **Writing Activities**   **Resources**

1

2   **Have handbooks available for children to examine and enjoy!**

3

Journal writing can be introduced anytime and should be continued throughout the year. .... HB (pp. 38-39)
PG (The Forms of Writing, pp. 3-7)

4   **Introducing the Handbook** .... HB (All sections)
PG (Getting Started Activities, pp. 4-12)

5   Continued from the previous week.
The activities for "Jenny Writes/ Being a Writer" could be the focus for this week. .... HB (pp. 10-21)
PG (The Process of Writing, pp. 3-8)

6   **Writing Friendly Notes** .... HB (pp. 42-43)
PG (The Forms of Writing, pp. 13-16)

7   **Making Alphabet Books** .... HB (pp. 66-67)
PG (The Forms of Writing, pp. 61-65)

8   Continued from the previous week.
Encourage children to use "Alphabet Sounds and Words" as a resource for their alphabet books. .... HB (pp. 96-121)

Special Note: **Use handbook chapters and activities in "Reading and Word Study" and "The Student Almanac" sections as ongoing resources throughout the year.**

HB—*Write One* Student Handbook
PG—*Language Series Program Guide* (Ring Binder)

Week **Writing Activities**   **Resources**

1   **Writing Lists** . . . . HB (pp. 40-41)
                                                        PG (The Forms of Writing, pp. 9-12)

2   **Writing Sentences** . . . . HB (p. 28)
                                                        PG (The Process of Writing, pp. 19-21
                                                            and p. 35)

      and

      Using End Punctuation . . . . HB (p. 32)
                                                        PG (The Process of Writing, p. 26
                                                            and p. 38)

3   **Writing Captions** . . . . HB (pp. 56-57)
                                                        PG (The Forms of Writing, pp. 45-48)

4   **Writing with Patterns** . . . . HB (pp. 78-79)
                                                        PG (The Forms of Writing, pp. 83-87)

5   Continued from the previous week.

6   **Writing Directions** . . . . HB (pp. 54-55)
                                                        PG (The Forms of Writing, pp. 39-43)

7   **Writing Poems** . . . . HB (pp. 74-77)
                                                        PG (The Forms of Writing, pp. 77-81)

8   Continued from the previous week.

Special Note: **Use handbook chapters and activities in "Reading and Word Study"**
             and "The Student Almanac" sections as ongoing resources
             throughout the year.

HB—*Write One* Student Handbook
PG—*Language Series Program Guide* (Ring Binder)

Week	Writing Activities	Resources
1	Writing Friendly Letters	HB (pp. 44-45) PG (The Forms of Writing, pp. 17-21)
2	Steps in the Writing Process	HB (pp. 22-25) PG (The Process of Writing, pp. 9-15)
3	Writing Stories About Me	HB (pp. 46-47) PG (The Forms of Writing, pp. 23-27)
4	Continued from the previous week.	
5	Using Capital Letters/ Making Plurals	HB (pp. 30-31) PG (The Process of Writing, pp. 22-25 and pp. 36-37)
6	Writing About Others	HB (pp. 50-51) PG (The Forms of Writing, pp. 29-33)
	or	
	Writing a Description	HB (pp. 52-53) PG (The Forms of Writing, pp. 35-38)
7	Continued from the previous week.	
8	Using Punctuation	HB (p. 33) PG (The Process of Writing, pp. 27-28 and p. 38)
	You may choose to use "Writing About Books" anytime.	HB (pp. 58-59) PG (The Forms of Writing, pp. 49-53)

Special Note: **Use handbook chapters and activities in "The Process of Writing" section and continue to use all sections of the handbook as regular resources.**

Write One Yearlong Timetable of Units   FOURTH QUARTER

HB—*Write One* Student Handbook
PG—*Language Series Program Guide* (Ring Binder)

Week	Writing Activities	Resources

1 **Writing Reports** . . . . HB (pp. 62-65)
PG (The Forms of Writing, pp. 55-59)

2 Continued from the previous week.

3 Continued from the previous week.

*You may choose to use "Writing in
Learning Logs" anytime* . . . . HB (pp. 68-69)
PG (The Forms of Writing, pp. 67-70)

4 **Understanding Our Language** . . . . HB (pp. 34-35)
PG (The Process of Writing, pp. 29-34
and pp. 39-40)

5 **Writing Stories**. . . . . HB (pp. 72-73)
PG (The Forms of Writing, pp. 71-76)

6 Continued from the previous week.

7 Continued from the previous week.

8 **Writers' Fest**

*Children can share their stories and reports and discuss what they've learned
about writing during the year.*

Special Note: **Use handbook chapters and activities in "The Process of Writing"
section and continue to use all sections of the handbook as regular
resources.**

The **PROCESS** of Writing

"The Process of Writing" section in *Write One* contains information that most of your students will be learning for the first time. With the exception of the story "Jenny Writes," you probably will not use this section until later in the school year. The more experience children have with beginning writing activities, the better they will be able to understand the process of writing.

All About Writing

Jenny Writes/Being a Writer

(handbook pages 10-21)

Young children have lots to tell you and, therefore, lots to write about. They simply need to learn about and practice being writers. In the story "Jenny Writes," students meet four children who are involved in the writing process. Of the four, Jenny can't find an idea for writing, but through sharing with her classmates, and seeing them writing, she eventually decides to write a note to her parents.

Immediately following "Jenny Writes" is a two-page commentary on the message of the story. It presents five things you do when you write: (1) Gather your materials. (2) Write about things you know about. (3) Learn to use the writing process. (4) Find ways to spell. (5) Share your writing with others.

Rationale

✔ **Young learners are at many different levels of writing ability.**

✔ **No matter what their present competency, learning about the writing process will help young students improve as writers.**

Major Concepts

✱ Writers use various materials. (pages 10-21)

✱ Writers write about things they know about. (pages 12, 14, 20)

✱ Writers help each other by sharing ideas. (pages 10-21)

✱ Writers find ways to spell words. (page 21)

✱ Writers can learn to use the writing process. (pages 10-21)

✱ Writers can and should share their writing with others. (pages 10-21)

Planning Notes

Materials: Writing materials

Steps in the Writing Process

(handbook pages 22-25)

Young children learn to write through imitation and instruction. At an early age they begin to experiment with pens, pencils, crayons, markers, and even keyboards. After a while, children learn that writing is much more than making marks on paper. They must grow into writing words, sentences, paragraphs, and then move on to the different forms of writing.

In this chapter, children learn that the writing process involves planning, writing, revising, checking, and publishing. A sample piece of writing is used to show each step in the process.

Rationale

✔ **Young writers learn through imitation and instruction.**

✔ **Children can learn to use the writing process to advance their composing skills.**

Major Concepts

✱ Planning writing can involve talking, drawing, thinking, and listing. (page 22)

✱ Writing a first draft means putting ideas about a topic into sentences. (page 23)

✱ Revising means making changes to make writing clear and accurate. (page 24)

✱ Students should check their writing for correct capitalization, punctuation, and spelling. (page 24)

✱ Publishing means making a final copy and sharing a piece of writing. (page 25)

Planning Notes

Materials: Writing materials

Professional Connections: Read the chapters related to the writing process in Carol Avery's book . . . *And with a Light Touch: Learning About Reading, Writing, and Teaching with First Graders* (Heinemann, 1993).

Rules for Writing

*(handbook
pages 27-35)*

Young learners are often effective oral communicators even before they enter school. After all, they have had "years" of experience developing their speaking abilities. However, written communication is new to most beginning students. They need to gain a basic understanding of sentences, mechanics, and grammar (parts of speech) in order to develop their writing abilities.

The "Rules for Writing" section in the handbook covers these basics—from writing sentences to making plurals, from using punctuation to understanding parts of speech. When you are ready to introduce your students to the basic rules for writing, this section will serve as the perfect starting point.

Rationale

✔ **Beginning writers need to learn the basic rules for writing.**

✔ **Students should know that following certain rules will help them clearly communicate their thoughts in writing.**

Major Concepts

✳ Writers use sentences to express their ideas. (page 28)

✳ The three basic types of sentences are telling sentences, asking sentences, and feeling sentences. (page 29)

✳ Capital letters are used at the beginning of sentences, for names, and for the word *I*. (page 30)

✳ Most plurals are formed by adding "s" or "es" to a word. (page 31)

✳ End punctuation marks (periods, question marks, and exclamation points) show where sentences end. (page 32)

✳ Commas keep the words in a sentence from running together. (page 33)

✳ Apostrophes show left-out letters or ownership. (page 33)

✳ Quotation marks are used to punctuate dialogue. (page 33)

✳ Four basic parts of speech are nouns, pronouns, verbs, and adjectives. (pages 34-35)

Planning Notes

Handbook Connections:
"Jenny Writes," pages 10-19
"Being a Writer," pages 20-21
"Steps in the Writing Process," pages 22-25

The **FORMS** of Writing

You can build a timely and comprehensive writing program around "The Forms of Writing" section in *Write One*. Included in this section of the handbook are guidelines for writing journals, lists, friendly letters, poems, stories, and much more.

Personal Writing

Subject Writing

Research Writing

Story and Poetry Writing

Writing in Journals

*(handbook
pages 38-39)*

Journal writing can be an integral part of the language arts curriculum. In the beginning, it's important to model the journal-writing process. Though ability levels may vary greatly at the start of the school year, most children have some knowledge of letter sounds and are able to approximate words. Children who sound out words begin to generalize spelling rules. However, in journal writing, the freedom to express ideas naturally is more important than accurate spelling.

Journal writing offers children opportunities to improve their reading and writing fluency. When children reread their journal writing, they discover the satisfaction of capturing important ideas and memories in writing.

Rationale

✔ **Daily journal writing improves children's confidence in their writing ability.**

✔ **The quality of children's writing improves only with practice.**

✔ **Receiving encouragement for personal writing promotes enthusiasm for writing in general.**

Major Concepts

✱ Journals are places to write about things you do and think about. (page 38)

✱ Children should write in their journals daily. (page 38)

✱ Journals can be used for recording many types of information. (page 39)

Planning Notes

Materials: Blank books or notebooks, paper, pencils, crayons, date stamp

Across-the-Curriculum Connections: Journals and learning logs can be used in any subject area for problem solving and for recording observations, thoughts, opinions, and reflections.

Writing Lists

*(handbook
pages 40-41)*

Children often see parents and other adults writing lists: gift lists, grocery lists, things-to-do-today lists. They observe that lists can be used for many things. In this unit, children will find that they can write their own lists, discovering that doing so is not only purposeful, but also enjoyable.

Rationale

✔ **Lists help students categorize and group.**

✔ **Lists help children become organized.**

✔ **Lists can provide writing ideas.**

Major Concepts

✱ There are many kinds of lists. (pages 40-41)

✱ Lists can show what you know. (page 40)

✱ Lists can help you remember. (page 41)

✱ Lists can be fun. (pages 40-41)

Planning Notes

Materials: Writing implements, chart paper or chalkboard, writing paper, art supplies

Handbook Connections:
"List Poem," page 77
"Using Everyday Words," pages 86-89
"Alphabet Sounds and Words," pages 96-121
"Calendar Words," page 133
"Weather Words," page 137
"Animals of the . . . ," pages 144-145

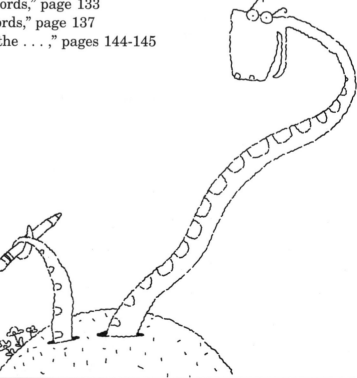

Writing Friendly Notes

(handbook pages 42-43)

The appeal of friendly notes is tremendous. Children love to send and receive notes. "Writing Friendly Notes" encourages students to write notes for fun. Two models, an invitation and a thank-you note, demonstrate how simple the messages can be.

Rationale

✔ **Writing friendly notes is a common way for children to send messages to other people.**

✔ **The usually swift response from those who receive notes encourages students to keep writing.**

Major Concepts

✱ **Writing a friendly note is fun.** (page 42)

✱ **People use friendly notes for invitations, thank-you notes, and other communications.** (pages 42-43)

Planning Notes

Materials: A supply of appealing stationery, small notepaper, construction paper, colored pencils, pens, rubber stamps, stickers

Reading-Writing Connections: Set up mailboxes for each child (and yourself) in your classroom. On a special day, write a note to each child. This can be the beginning of a flurry of note writing that goes on all year between everyone in the classroom community. (Be sure children understand that mailbox names are listed in ABC order.)

School Connections: Children can send their notes to members of the greater school community. Consider different note-writing opportunities: thank-you notes to helpers, invitations to class events, or happy notes.

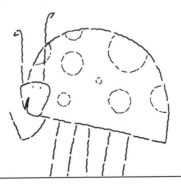

Writing Friendly Letters

(handbook pages 44-45)

"Writing Friendly Letters" shows students how to write to someone near or faraway. This chapter includes a model letter, with its five parts highlighted, and a model envelope, also clearly labeled.

Rationale

✔ **Writing friendly letters is an important social skill.**

✔ **Friendly letters to communicate news, express thanks, and so on, provide relaxed writing experiences.**

Major Concepts

✳ Friendly letters can reach friends and relatives near and faraway. (page 44)

✳ There are five parts to a friendly letter: date, greeting, message, closing, and the writer's name. (page 44)

✳ The envelope must include the sender's address, a mailing address, and a stamp. (page 45)

Planning Notes

Materials: Stationery and envelopes of different sizes and colors, pens, colored pencils, rubber stamps, stickers

Reading-Writing Connections: Children can write to favorite authors, asking them questions and telling them what they like about their books. (Direct these letters to the authors in care of their publisher's address.)

School and Community Connections: Students can use friendly letters to communicate with members of their community. They might write a note of thanks after a memorable field trip or assembly. Also consider using the friendly-letter format to encourage young reporters. They can share news from your classroom with the whole school via a letter to the school newsletter editor.

Technology Connections: Many children's word-processing programs have "print shop" features that are a natural match for friendly-letter writing. Take time to teach your class how to type their friendly letters on the computer. Often they will have choices of fonts, pictures, and borders to personalize their letters.

Writing Stories About Me

*(handbook
pages 46-47)*

"Writing Stories About Me" will help young writers express themselves, using their own experiences. Books, pictures, lists, and class sharing time will all be used to show children how to choose a subject, make a plan, and write their stories.

Rationale

✔ Stories based on personal experience provide a natural starting point for young first-time writers.

✔ All children have had experiences, and most are motivated to share them.

✔ A "story about me" gives the writer a feeling of ownership.

Major Concepts

* "Stories about me" tell about the writer's experience. (page 46)

* Students can learn to plan and write stories about their experiences, using clusters. (pages 46-47)

Planning Notes

Materials: Books and stories to share about other children's experiences; paper, pencils, art materials; pictures of families, sports, animals, foods, etc.

School and Community Connections: Invite students to write about their interests, things they do with their families, and likes and dislikes. These stories may be shared within the classroom or in the community via school or local newspapers.

Science Connections: Stories about foods, caring for animals, and tending plants can be linked to science topics. Focus on good observation skills using the five senses (handbook pages 146-147).

Social Studies Connections: Personal stories with a cultural basis fit well with a unit on ethnic awareness and customs. Emphasize respect for individual differences as well as appreciation of others' similar likes, abilities, and needs.

A Happy Day

One day baby Josh came home. He was in a yellow blanket. My mom let me hold him. He was blowing ... He didn't cry.

Writing About Others

*(handbook
pages 50-51)*

Writing about someone they know well is often a successful experience for young writers. They have lots of details to draw on as starting points for descriptions of favorite friends, neighbors, or relatives. Their writings can be funny, sad, exciting, etc.

For another approach, children can research and write about important or famous people.

Rationale

✔ **Writing about others draws on children's own experiences and relationships.**

✔ **Children enjoy telling others about people they know.**

✔ **Children learn to look beyond themselves when they write about others.**

Major Concepts

✱ Children have many subjects to choose from when writing about others. (pages 50-51)

✱ Young writers learn how to begin with an important idea and add details. (page 50)

Planning Notes

Materials: Paper, pencils, puppets, books with a specific character and a predictable text (such as Mem Fox's *Tough Boris*), special-interest filmstrips or videos, biographies, an overhead projector

Social Studies Connections: Children can read about well-known people or a favorite author. They can use the information they gather to plan a dramatization or a puppet show.

Writing a Description

(handbook pages 52-53)

In this chapter, children are encouraged to use their five senses—seeing, hearing, touching, tasting, and smelling—to describe people and objects. As they learn to observe carefully, through their senses, students will find the words and phrases they need for their writing.

Rationale

✔ **Writing descriptions of familiar people, places, animals, and things taps the full resource of personal experience.**

✔ **Using their senses, children find the details needed for description writing.**

Major Concepts

✱ Children share their own experiences when they write descriptions. (pages 52-53)

✱ Writing a description involves telling how something or someone feels, tastes, looks, sounds, and/or smells. (pages 52-53)

Planning Notes

Materials: A bag with a piece of fruit in it; popcorn (popped) for students; paper, pencils, art materials

Handbook Connections:
"Five Senses," pages 146-147
"Writing in Journals," pages 38-39
"Writing in Learning Logs," pages 68-69

Science Connections: Successful learning using hands-on experiments depends upon good observation skills. Children can use their senses to understand and describe these activities. Such experiments also provide opportunities for recording information in journals and learning logs.

Our New Car

Our new car is green.
It has a sunroof.
It has soft tan seats.
It is sporty.
My dad thinks it's cool.

Writing Directions

(handbook pages 54-55)

Writing directions is an excellent way for children to share their interests and skills with others. It is also the perfect opportunity to learn about ordering information in a step-by-step sequence. Such logical presentation of details will be useful to young students in all future writing tasks.

Rationale

✔ **Learning to put details in good order is basic to written communication.**

✔ **Writing directions is a natural way to learn step-by-step sequencing.**

Major Concepts

✳ **Children can identify the steps required to do a familiar task. (page 54)**

✳ **Children can share the steps in proper sequence by using words (*first, next, then*) or numbers (1, 2, 3). (pages 54-55)**

Planning Notes

Materials: Paper, pencils, materials or pictures to sequence, manipulatives, chart paper, markers, classroom rules and procedures

Math Connections: After using manipulatives to solve a problem, the steps taken to reach the solution can be listed. (The problem is "10 − 3 = ?" First, I put down 10 chips. Next, I take away 3. Then, I count how many are left to find the answer, 7.)

Science Connections: The science options are endless since most experiments are set up in a step-by-step sequence.

Social Studies Connections: Write directions about making friends or helping others, rules for a safe playground time, recipes from other lands, and so on. These can be completed as posters and put up around your school.

Writing Captions

*(handbook
pages 56-57)*

There are many opportunities for writing captions in a classroom and throughout a school building. Captions make pictures and bulletin boards more interesting and informative. They are also a good starting place for young writers. When a caption is posted, it can easily grow into a longer sentence. It may even become the start of a good story.

Rationale

✔ **Captions add information and interest to an environment.**

✔ **Writing captions is meaningful writing for young learners.**

✔ **Captions encourage reading and writing.**

Major Concepts

✳ Captions add interest to pictures. (page 56)

✳ Captions give special information. (page 57)

Planning Notes

Materials: Camera, film, magazines, construction paper, markers, stapler, writing implements, paper, strips of poster paper

Health Connections: Have students create pictures of healthful meals directly on paper plates. After choosing the foods, they can either paste pictures or draw their own onto the plate. Then ask them to make up captions for their meals and write them on slips of paper to attach somewhere on the plate. (During this activity, refer students to the food pyramid on pages 142-143 of their handbooks.)

MIGRATION

Butterflies move from place to place.

Writing About Books

(handbook pages 58-59)

Many children have a favorite story they love to hear . . . and tell. Many children also have a particular book they enjoy reading and talking about. They often know the author and can tell you why they like the book. In a sense, it is natural for children to "sell" their favorite books, convincing others to read them, too. And this is what they'll be doing when they write about books.

Rationale

✔ Children can motivate others to read books.

✔ Writing about books helps children think creatively and critically.

✔ Writing and telling about books demonstrate comprehension of text.

Major Concepts

✱ Reading books and writing about them can be fun. (page 58)

✱ You can write about books in creative ways. (pages 58-59)

✱ You can also tell about books. (page 59)

Planning Notes

Materials: A supply of favorite books, writing and art materials, large paper grocery bags, poster board or chart paper

Handbook Connections:
"Writing Poems," pages 74-77
"Reading to Understand," pages 82-83

Reading-Writing Connections: Encourage children to write the titles, authors, and a sentence or two about their favorite books in their journals. This will give them material for writing about books at another time.

Book ___Three Ducks Went Wandering___

by ___Ron Roy___

One sunny day
the ducks ran away.
They wanted to play.

Writing Reports

(handbook pages 62-65)

Children are eager and excited to learn and talk about things that interest them. "Writing Reports" will help them write about interesting topics as well.

They will find out how to plan first and then will proceed through the writing, revising, checking, and publishing stages of the writing process.

Rationale

✔ **Students have many interests and often know a lot about these subjects.**

✔ **Students can learn more about these subjects in school.**

✔ **Writing a report is one way for students to share their knowledge.**

Major Concepts

✱ Planning—learning and listing important facts—is the first step in writing a report. (page 62)

✱ Students choose key facts from their lists and write sentences. (page 63)

✱ To revise, students read their reports and change anything that doesn't sound right. (page 64)

✱ Checking involves looking for errors in punctuation, capitals, and spelling. (page 64)

✱ Children publish reports by making a neat copy to share. (page 65)

Planning Notes

Materials: Writing materials; crayons or markers; books, magazines, videos, etc., on a variety of topics (animals, places, hobbies, sports, famous people—choose these according to your children's interests)

Handbook Connections:
"Steps in the Writing Process," pages 22-25
"Rules for Writing" section, pages 27-35

Across-the-Curriculum Connections: Current units in science, social studies, and geography may present topics perfect for first-time reports. Keep your eyes and ears open for students' interests.

Making Alphabet Books

(handbook pages 66-67)

Most young children are able to sing and recite the alphabet from early childhood. Gradually they learn to identify letters by name and sound. In this chapter, children will learn that the alphabet can be used as a planning tool for writing—especially for making picture dictionaries. Fun awaits them as they collaborate on this accessible form of writing!

Rationale

✔ **Working with the alphabet expands children's reading and writing abilities.**

✔ **An alphabet book can be a cooperative venture for the whole class.**

✔ **Alphabet books are tools for exploring ideas, and can be either serious or silly.**

Major Concepts

✳ Writing alphabet books fosters creativity and cooperation among classmates. (pages 66-67)

✳ Alphabet books expand children's vocabularies. (page 66)

Planning Notes

Materials: Several alphabet books to share, writing materials, large chart paper, magazines and newspapers

Science Connections: Insects, animals, plants, oceans, and deserts are all rich subject matter for alphabet books. Try to get copies of the ABC-book series about science by Jerry Pallota (Charlesbridge Publishers) to read with your students.

Social Studies Connections: Make school alphabet books, community or neighborhood alphabet books, alphabet books about cities, family celebrations, farms, etc.

Words About Our School

A art	G gym
B bus	H heart
C calendar	I ice cream
D dancing	J jokes
E Eastview	K kindness
F friends	L lunch

Writing in Learning Logs

*(handbook
pages 68-69)*

"Writing in Learning Logs" will introduce children to a personal way of enhancing their classroom learning. A good method for tracking long-term projects, these logs can be used to make observations, ask questions, and record facts. Students can also benefit from daily class-wide use of learning logs—jotting down questions or problems from math class, noting new or unfamiliar words, recording an interesting detail learned in social studies, and so on.

Rationale

✔ Learning logs help children chart sequential progress of an activity, as well as make predictions about what may occur.

✔ Learning logs involve the students, making learning a lasting, personal experience.

✔ Information collected in a learning log can be used in reports.

Major Concepts

✳ Learning logs can be used to report on projects or activities occurring in the classroom. (pages 68-69)

✳ Students' learning is reinforced by writing down observations and questions about class work. (page 69)

Planning Notes

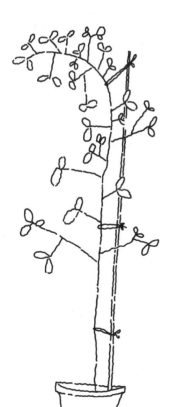

Materials: Notebooks or stapled paper to form logs, pencils, crayons, measuring tools

Science Connections: Logs can be used to report on projects involving plants or animals, the five senses, the main food groups, weather and seasons, etc.

Math Connections: Learning logs lend themselves to various math-based activities (recording steps, dating log entries, making measurements, etc.).

Classroom Connections: Sending learning logs home is a good way to let families know what children have learned.

Writing Stories

(handbook pages 72-73)

"Writing Stories" introduces children to two simple elements of the story—characters and something happening. A model story, "Pumpkin the Cat," demonstrates these elements and the fact that a story has a beginning, a middle, and an ending. It is interesting to note that these same elements are already evident in the stories that young children tell so naturally. Their storytelling and picture-making abilities will take them to the next step of becoming story writers.

Rationale

✔ **Children are imaginative and spontaneous storytellers.**

✔ **Young writers can use their oral language and art abilities to plan their stories.**

✔ **Firsthand experience with books and stories is the best preparation for writing stories.**

Major Concepts

✱ There are different ways to plan a story. (page 72)

✱ You can answer questions about the characters and what happens. (page 72)

✱ You can tell a story by making a picture. (page 72)

✱ A story has a beginning, a middle, and an ending. (page 73)

Planning Notes

Materials: Writing materials, favorite storybooks, art materials

Reading-Writing Connections: Classrooms and homes where children hear stories and are surrounded by storybooks are the places where story writing begins. Be sure your classroom is this kind of place.

School-Home Connections: If possible, have a checkout procedure so that children may take favorite storybooks home. Read about WEB, a systematic procedure for classroom checkout and return of books, in Regie Routman's book *Invitations* (Heinemann, 1991; 1994).

Writing Poems

*(handbook
pages 74-77)*

Young children respond naturally to the rhythm, rhyme, and images of poetry. In this chapter, students are introduced to poems that rhyme as well as to simpler structures like list poems. Models written by children demonstrate that poetry can be written and enjoyed by early readers and writers.

Rationale

✔ Short poems are perfect fare for beginning readers and writers.

✔ Writing poems provides practice in using specific language.

✔ Poetry adds fun and variety to early language arts classes.

Major Concepts

✱ Writing poems is like making word pictures. (page 74)

✱ Various forms of poetry use rhyming words. (pages 74-75)

✱ Some poems have a simple structure that is easy to imitate. (pages 76-77)

Planning Notes

Materials: Poetry books and anthologies, songs, chart paper, writing and art materials

Music Connections: Play instrumental music or have children play rhythm instruments during poetry readings. Write new verses to songs.

Choral Readings: Many poems can be arranged as choral readings. You may divide favorite poems (including original ones) according to the following categories: solo, groups one and two, and all together.

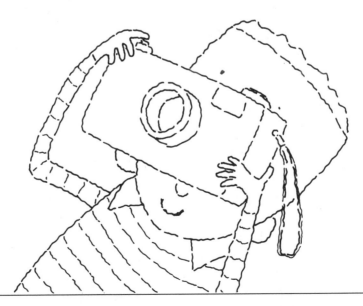

Writing with Patterns

(handbook pages 78-79)

Stories and songs written with patterns of rhythm, repetition, and rhyme readily engage readers—and writers. Texts like "Brown Bear, Brown Bear" by Bill Martin, Jr., and "Down by the Bay" by Raffi encourage early success in reading, and are easily modeled by beginning writers. Pattern books and songs also encourage group participation and are lots of fun.

Rationale

✔ **Pattern songs and stories engage early readers and writers.**

✔ **Children at all levels can recognize and imitate the patterns in stories, songs, and poems.**

Major Concepts

✳ Children are able to identify the rhyme and beat in the songs and stories they hear, read, and write. (pages 78-79)

✳ After exposure to predictable texts, children can write their own. (page 79)

Planning Notes

Materials: Several types of pattern stories, chart paper, writing and drawing materials

Math Connections: There are many patterns and predictable outcomes in math. Children can find number patterns when they work with manipulatives and charts. Look at the hundred chart on page 154. Help the children discover the obvious patterns of 1's, 5's, and 10's. See if they can discover other patterns on their own.

Science Connections: The study of weather lends itself to finding and discussing patterns. Use pages 136-137 in the handbook to talk about the weather patterns of each season; the sky, wind, and air before and during rainstorms, snowstorms, or violent storms; lightning and thunder; and any other weather or seasonal patterns children have noticed.

Reading and
WORD STUDY

The "Reading and Word Study" handbook section gives students various opportunities to find and explore words related to early reading and writing. Besides a short chapter addressing reading comprehension, you'll find a number of useful word lists that children can refer to as they work toward greater independence in their language arts learning.

Reading Skills

Reading to Understand

*(handbook
pages 82-83)*

Appropriate reading instruction for young children is founded on exposure to well-written books and texts and on meaningful reading activities. Good instruction begins before children even open a book, continues during their reading, and follows it as well.

Before-reading activities involve discussions about prior knowledge of a topic, an introduction to important concepts in the book (if needed), and reminders about the purpose of the reading. Activities during reading involve metacognitive behaviors, and activities after reading involve reflection and assimilation.

Rationale

✔ **Reading to understand should be the primary goal of readers and reading instruction.**

✔ **Using strategies before, during, and after reading helps young children grow into thoughtful readers.**

✔ **Reading strategies can be modeled naturally during children's reading time.**

Major Concepts

✱ Readers should think before, during, and after reading. (pages 82-83)

✱ Readers can do certain things before, during, and after reading to help them become readers who understand. (pages 82-83)

Planning Notes

Materials: A collection of appropriate reading materials

Handbook Connections:
"Reading New Words," pages 84-85
"Using the Right Word," pages 90-93

Reading New Words

(handbook pages 84-85)

As children grow into reading, they regularly come across unfamiliar words. There are many ways to foster independence in word recognition, which in turn increases reading ease and enjoyment for these young learners. First, it is important that they know how to use context and pictures as clues. It is also important for them to know how to look at words, to find patterns, and to attempt new words, using the sounds they know. Finally, children should feel free to ask for help—for the actual pronunciation of a word, or for a strategy to figure out the word!

Rationale

✔ **Young readers need to learn strategies for reading new words.**

✔ **As children become more independent readers, their enjoyment of reading increases.**

Major Concepts

✱ There are many ways to read new words. (pages 84-85)

✱ Using context clues, letter patterns, and sound-symbol relationships are three important ways of approaching new words. (pages 84-85)

Planning Notes

Materials: Reading materials that both match and challenge your students' reading abilities

Technology Connections: The Learning Company, Edmark Corporation, and Brøderbund publish computer programs that involve young children in word-building activities.

Handbook Connections:
"Reading to Understand," pages 82-83
"Using Everyday Words," pages 86-89
"Word-Study Skills" section, pages 95-129

Using Everyday Words

*(handbook
pages 86-89)*

The list of "everyday words" includes many that are most frequently used by writers (and readers). The words appear in alphabetical order as a ready spelling reference for children, although this list is not meant to be used as the core of a spelling program. Close to the beginning of the yellow-edged section of the handbook, these handy pages are easy to find.

Rationale

✔ Beginning writers need ready references for writing/spelling words.

✔ The English language has a relatively small core of "most frequently used" words.

Major Concepts

✱ Everyday words are words you read and write many times a day. (pages 86-89)

✱ Alphabetical lists of words make a ready reference for beginning writers. (pages 86-89)

Planning Notes

Handbook Connections:
"Making Alphabet Books," pages 66-67
"Reading New Words," pages 84-85
"Using the Right Word," pages 90-93

Using the Right Word

(handbook pages 90-93)

Words that sound the same but have different meanings are called homophones. Most of these distinctions are beyond the grasp of early writers. There are, however, some homophones (four/for, no/know, red/read) that are a regular part of their reading and writing. These and a few other common ones are presented in the handbook.

Rationale

✔ **Children regularly meet homophones in their reading and writing.**

Major Concepts

✱ **Homophones are words that sound the same but have different meanings.** (page 90)

✱ **Some homophones are a regular part of young children's reading and writing.** (pages 90-93)

Word-Study Skills

*(handbook
pages 95-129)*

When children read, they need to be able to recognize words and know their meanings. For reading comprehension, these two processes must go on simultaneously. Using sound-symbol relationships is one of the ways to approach word recognition.

This word-study section includes a page for each letter of the alphabet, a highlighted key word, a colorful illustration, and a list of words focusing on a particular letter. The alphabet is followed by pages that address consonant blends and digraphs, short and long vowels, rhyming word families, contractions, and compound words.

Rationale

✔ **Reading well advances students' learning in all areas.**

✔ **Knowing the alphabet and its sound-symbol relationships facilitates word recognition.**

Major Concepts

✱ The English language uses alphabet letters and sounds to make words. (pages 96-121)

✱ Consonant sounds include initial and final sounds, blends, and digraphs. (pages 122-123)

✱ Vowel sounds include short and long sounds. (pages 124-125)

✱ Rhyming families help children learn many new words. (pages 126-127)

✱ Contractions and compound words have predictable structures. (pages 128-129)

Planning Notes

Handbook Connections:
"Reading to Understand," pages 82-83
"Reading New Words," pages 84-85
"Using Everyday Words," pages 86-89
"Using the Right Word," pages 90-93

Reading and Word Study 57

Handbook MINILESSONS

Minilessons can transform any classroom into an active learning environment. (We define a minilesson as instruction that lasts about 15-20 minutes and covers a single idea or a core of basic information.) Minilessons can be delivered from the front of the room and include the entire class. They can also be individualized or implemented in writing groups. Ideally, each lesson will address a specific need your students have at a particular time. This makes the lesson meaningful and successful.

In this section, there are minilessons listed for most of the chapters in the handbook. You will find these short exercises invaluable as you plan activities related to the handbook. An answer key for those minilessons that call for specific answers begins on page 87.

The Process of Writing

I like spaghetti. . . . . **Writing Sentences**

READ and **DISCUSS** the three different kinds of sentences on page 29. **FOCUS** on the asking sentence. **ASK** children to copy the following sentence (question) onto a half piece of paper and then answer it with as many words as they can.

    What do you like to eat?

Happy Birthday! . . . . **Writing Sentences**

WRITE the following sentences without end punctuation on the chalkboard:

Is today your birthday	Wow, I love presents
Yes	How old are you
This present is for you	I'm seven years old

REFER to handbook page 29 and **DISCUSS** the different kinds of sentences. Then **ASK** children to name the kind for each sentence on the board. Let volunteers **ADD** the ending punctuation for each sentence. Finally, **INVITE** pairs of children to take turns reading the sentences as a dialogue.

Color the capital. . . . . **Using Capital Letters**

REMIND children that sentences and names begin with capital letters. **WRITE** the following sentences on the board:

my kitten is funny.	the dog's name is moppy.
do you like him?	she lives in florida.
billy and ty have a dog.	

INVITE volunteers to put the capital letters in with colored chalk. **HAVE** them tell why a capital letter is needed.

People We Know . . . . **Using Capital Letters**

READ page 30 with the children. **WRITE** the names of several members of the school staff or community, in lowercase, on the chalkboard. **ASK** students to rewrite the names correctly. This can be done individually or as a class activity.

Make More . . . . **Making Plurals**

ASK children to draw pictures for the following words:

hats   pans   flags

REMIND them that the "s" at the end makes these words plural. What does this mean about their pictures?

Just One More . . . . **Making Plurals**

DISCUSS the rules for making plurals on page 31 in the handbook. Then **ASK** children to turn to page 106 in the yellow section of their book, the "Kk" page. **EXPLAIN** that all of the words there are singular, refer to one thing. **TELL** students to make a list of the plurals of these words by adding "s" or "es."

Holiday Marks . . . . **Using End Marks**

On the chalkboard **WRITE** the following sentences and **READ** them with your students:

Thanksgiving comes in the fall
What are you thankful for
I love Thanksgiving Day
What holiday do you like

ASK students to decide which punctuation mark is needed at the end of each sentence. Then **CALL ON** volunteers to come to the board and add them.

Questions and Answers . . . . **Using End Marks**

WRITE the following questions and answers on the chalkboard:

Where is Vito	He's reading a joke book
Do you see him	He's in the yard
Why is he laughing	No, I don't

ASK for volunteers to put the correct punctuation mark after each sentence. Then **HAVE** them match the questions with the correct answers.

I like . . . . **Using Commas**

READ about commas on page 33. Then **DISCUSS** the use of commas in a series. **WRITE** a sentence on the chalkboard about three things you like, but **LEAVE OUT** the commas. **ASK** for volunteers to put the commas where they belong. Then **HAVE** children write their own "I like" sentences.

Who said it? . . . . **Using Quotation Marks**

CHOOSE a well-known story with plenty of dialogue. **POINT OUT** how the author uses quotation marks to show that characters are talking. **HAVE** children read the words within the quotation marks. Then **ASK** them to find out who is doing the talking. As a follow-up, **TELL** children to write two sentences using this pattern:

I said, " ."
Then my friend said, " ."

Noun Hunt . . . . **Nouns**

TURN to any one of the alphabet pages in the yellow section of the handbook, beginning on page 96. **TELL** children that most of these words are naming words, or nouns. **TALK ABOUT** whether each word is a person, a place, or a thing. **REPEAT** this activity with other alphabet pages.

Person, Place, or Thing . . . . **Nouns**

On the chalkboard **MAKE** a chart like the one below. Then **ASK** children to call out words for each category. **WRITE** them in the correct column. **EXPLAIN** that these words are all nouns. Also **POINT OUT** that the proper nouns begin with a capital letter.

Person	Place	Thing

Who is it? . . . . **Pronouns**

WRITE the following sentences on the chalkboard:

"Ellen is with <u>me</u>," said Mom.

"<u>I</u> like popcorn," said Jake.

There goes Kaz. <u>He</u> runs fast.

<u>Her</u> name is Shavon.

TELL children that the underlined words are called pronouns (check handbook page 34), and that pronouns take the place of nouns. **ASK** children to work with partners to figure out which noun each of the pronouns stands for. **SHARE** answers and discuss.

Act it out. . . . . **Verbs**

PREPARE cards with action words (*run, scratch, hop, wave, drink,* etc.) on them. **EXPLAIN** that these words are called verbs. **HAVE** children pick the verb cards from a hat and act them out for the class. The other children can guess the word. (Either have them guess the word verbally, or ask them to number their papers and write the verb for each actor.) This activity is fun for small groups.

Children can . . . . **Verbs**

READ about verbs on page 35. Then, to show the importance of verbs, **READ** both model sentences, leaving out the verbs. To further **SHOW** how verbs affect the meaning of sentences, **USE** the following model. See how many different verbs the children can find for this sentence pattern:

Children can _____ .

Beautiful Blue Ocean . . . . **Adjectives**

READ about adjectives on page 35. Then **ASK** children to turn to pages 138-139. **HELP** them to think of adjectives to describe the places shown there (mountains, forest, canyon, meadow, ocean, etc.). One thing they may remember from this activity is that color words are usually used as adjectives.

The Forms of Writing

Special Events . . . . **Writing in Journals**

ASK children to make journal entries whenever the class goes on a field trip, has a guest speaker, attends a special school assembly, or does an all-class project. **HAVE** the children date the entries. **INVITE** the children to make drawings of their favorite part of the activity. **DIRECT** them to write a sentence or two about their pictures.

One-Liners . . . . **Writing in Journals**

READ a story to the class. **HAVE** children enter the title and author of the story on a journal page. **INVITE** them to illustrate their favorite part of the story and then write one sentence about it.

End of the Day . . . . **Writing in Journals**

USE journals to "wrap up" the school day. **SUGGEST** that children write about the best part of their day. **ASK** them to select one of these wrap-up entries each week or so for you to **REPRODUCE** and send home.

Names . . . . **Writing Lists**

HAVE children make authentic lists of names, including who is going to read to the teacher, kids at a table, who is at the center, and so on. Names are powerful teaching tools!

Happy Words . . . . **Writing Lists**

READ and **DISCUSS** the lists on pages 40-41 in the handbook. **WRITE** a list of "Happy Words" with your class. **RECORD** the words on a chart as students suggest them to you. Then **ASK** students to choose two of the words, write them on paper, and draw pictures about them.

Your Name . . . . Writing Friendly Notes

DISCUSS the importance of writing names correctly. **TELL** children to be sure they know how to spell the name of the person they are writing to. Also, **EMPHASIZE** the placement and importance of their names when they sign their notes.

Friendly Lists . . . . Writing Friendly Notes

CREATE a list of reasons to write friendly notes and a list of people to write to. **POST** these lists by your mailboxes. **ENCOURAGE** children to add to the lists when they have new ideas.

Thank You . . . . Writing Friendly Notes

DISCUSS how the many members of your school community make it a good place to learn. **INVITE** each of the children to choose someone in the school to thank with a friendly note. Their notes will undoubtedly brighten people's days, and the children might receive a note in return!

Stationery Styles . . . . Writing Friendly Letters

PLAN time for students to create a supply of their own special stationery. **SHARE** some examples with them, including the use of monograms, nicknames, and full names. Children may also vary the size, shape, color, and borders of the paper to create their own unique style. (They may also use the "print shop" feature of a word-processing program.)

Dear Editor . . . . Writing Friendly Letters

CHOOSE some letters to the editor from your local newspaper or from children's magazines such as *Ladybug*, *Spider*, or *Highlights*. **READ** them with your class, discussing what the important messages are in each letter. **DISCUSS** how they could use friendly letters to convey their own opinions. Then **ENCOURAGE** individual students, or the whole class, to think about writing a letter to an editor.

Family Times . . . . **Writing Stories About Me**

READ or **TELL** a favorite story about families. **ASK** children what they do with their families to help, play, and share. **INVITE** them to tell about their families' favorite activities. **LIST** these on a chart to display in the classroom.

Something for You . . . . **Writing Stories About Me**

HELP the children **USE** their finished stories to make a keepsake poster or greeting card as a gift for their families.

Authors' Stories . . . . **Writing Stories About Me**

READ autobiographical stories like Patricia Polacco's *Thundercake* or Tomie dePaola's *The Art Lesson* to spark a discussion about ideas to use for story writing.

Who am I? . . . . **Writing About Others**

WRITE riddles about teachers or other adults in your school. **ASK** the students to guess who is being described in each riddle. An example:

> I see you on Tuesdays and Thursdays.
> We run and play together.
> I teach you how to exercise.
> Who am I?

ENCOURAGE students to write their own riddles about friends, familiar book characters, or well-known people in the community.

Puppet Show . . . . **Writing About Others**

INVITE children to dramatize their descriptions. **SUGGEST** that students work in pairs—each one playing the role of the person they wrote about. They need to *imagine* what might happen if the two people would meet. **ASK** the children to think of interesting circumstances that might bring the two people together: riding on a bus, sitting in the park, grocery shopping, watching a ball game, and so on. **GIVE** the students simple sock or stick puppets, so they can "talk" together.

Look and Listen . . . . **Writing a Description**

READ a favorite story. **ASK** the children to think of some describing words about the people and animals in the story. **WRITE** the name of a character on the chalkboard and **LIST** the words as the children offer them. This can be a good prewriting activity for writing descriptions or riddles.

Think Again . . . . **Writing a Description**

ASK the children to describe each object as if they were the creatures in the following situations:

   an ant describing a toothbrush

   a worm describing an apple

   a butterfly describing a flower

   an elephant describing a bird

   (another perspective of their choice)

Then have them write one of their descriptions.

What am I? . . . . **Writing a Description**

PLAY a guessing game. **TELL** children to pick something in or around the school and, without naming it, describe it. They should use as many of their senses as they can. **WRITE** the following leads to help them:

   It looks _____ .

   It sounds _____ .

   It feels _____ .

   It tastes _____ .

   It smells _____ .

After a child describes something, the rest of the class has a chance to guess the object. This game would be fun in groups of 6-8 children.

School Time . . . . **Writing Directions**

DISCUSS a classroom procedure with your students. Together, come up with directions to follow. **WRITE** these in list form and post in the room.

Example:

Doing My Work

1. Put my name on my paper.
2. Follow directions.
3. Get help if I need it.
4. Put my finished work in the work basket.

Everyday Stuff . . . . **Writing Directions**

WRITE directions on the chalkboard or chart paper with input from the class. **USE** a familiar task, like tying shoes or brushing teeth. **ASK** one student to pantomime the activity. **STOP** after each significant step and write what has happened. For example, (1) Put water on the toothbrush. If necessary, revise the information you have taken from the pantomime, making sure the directions are clear.

Rules of the Game . . . . **Writing Directions**

ASK all the students to write their version of the rules for the game hide-and-seek. **COMPARE** versions. **DISCUSS** the differences.

Mapmakers . . . . **Writing Captions**

MAKE a simple outline map of the classroom on poster board or on the chalkboard. **GATHER** the children together and **WRITE** descriptive names of classroom centers or areas on the map ("Quiet Reading Area," "All-Class Art Supplies," etc.). **PREPARE** a smaller, individual version of the map for each child, or let children create their own. **ASK** them to write a caption for the whole room.

Act it out. . . . . **Writing Captions**

INVITE a few children to pantomime active things they like to do. After each one finishes, **ASK** the observers to guess what activity the pantomime showed. **WRITE** the answers on the board. Then **SHOW** how their answers can become interesting captions. **REMIND** them that a caption is like a sign that gives a little information. An answer like "He's swimming" can become "Summer Fun" or "Cory loves swimming."

Bag it! . . . . **Writing About Books**

PROVIDE children with large paper grocery bags and **TELL** them to decorate them with the title, author, and an illustration from a favorite story. **SURPRISE** the customers at a local grocery store with these special totes. (Of course, you must set this up with the store manager—who can also provide you with the bags.)

Bookmarks . . . . **Writing About Books**

CUT strips of stiff paper for bookmarks. Then **SHOW** children how to create bookmarks that advertise a favorite book. **TELL** them to put the title and author on one side and to write one sentence about the book on the other side. For a nice touch, **ASK** them to decorate the bookmark with borders or small illustrations. Bookmarks could be given to the patrons of the school or public library.

From Facts to Sentences . . . . **Writing Reports**

WRITE some short factual phrases on the chalkboard. **ASK** students to make up sentences using the facts. Example:

Fact	Sentence
Rhinoceros—tiny eyes	The rhinoceros has tiny eyes.

Finding Facts . . . . **Writing Reports**

CHOOSE a subject and guide a class discussion about it. **LIST** the ideas and facts that are shared on the chalkboard. Then find a book or magazine that contains more information on the topic. **SHOW** the children how to find this information. **ADD** some "new" facts to your list. (Do this same lesson on another day with a different topic and a different type of source.)

Sights and Sounds . . . . **Writing Reports**

CHOOSE a report topic that could involve a field trip for gathering facts (zoo animals, clowns, farm life, harvest, etc.). **PLAN** a trip to the zoo, a farm, a circus, or other place where children can practice looking and listening for report facts. **EQUIP** each student with a notebook and pencil and guide the note taking. (Practice note taking before the trip. For example, **ASK** the children to look out the window. What is the weather like? Have them write a note about it.)

Line Up . . . . **Making Alphabet Books**

CALL children to line up in alphabetical order. **DO** this for walking to lunch, the bus, a special program, etc. To keep things fair, **BEGIN** with a different letter each time. (Go from that letter to Z and continue with A, B, C, etc.)

ABC Teams . . . . **Making Alphabet Books**

PLACE children in teams of three. **GIVE** each team a list of letters from A to Z. The task for the children is to write words related to a specific topic (science, math, social studies) for each letter of the alphabet. (You may supply the topic if necessary.) At another time, the teams can use these lists for making group books.

Our Class . . . . **Writing in Learning Logs**

DO a shared writing of classroom activities at the end of a week, a month, or at the end of a project. **PHOTOCOPY** the information and send it home to families.

Classroom Pets . . . . **Writing in Learning Logs**

If appropriate, **CONDUCT** a study of your classroom pet. Children can describe the pet, record feeding times and eating habits, sleep habits, play activities, and other pet-care details. Possible long-term projects:

* Eggs-to-tadpoles-to-frogs development
* Incubated hen's eggs—hatching process through week-old chick

The Seasons . . . . **Writing in Learning Logs**

Focusing on the present season, **GO** on a nature walk. **HELP** the children to notice how plants and animals adapt to the new season.

Shadows . . . . **Writing in Learning Logs**

On a sunny day, **TAKE** the class outside as early in the day as possible. **STAND** in a circle and **TRACE** the shadows of several children. **GUIDE** the discussion as you make measurements and observations, including the sun and its position in the sky. Back in the classroom, **HELP** the children make their learning-log entries. **REPEAT** the process at noon and at the end of the day, making the appropriate comparisons.

PLAN to repeat this activity during other seasons of the year.

New Endings . . . . Writing Stories

READ a familiar or favorite story to the children. **RECALL** the sequence of events, stressing the beginning, middle, and ending. Then **ASK** "what if" questions and **HAVE** children get into small groups to make up different endings. (This exercise helps make children aware of the beginning-middle-ending elements in stories.)

Making Books . . . . Writing Stories

INVITE children to transfer their stories to individual pages that can be illustrated and then bound together in a book. **SHOW** how they can choose one or two lines for each page and then illustrate that page. **HAVE** them complete the process by adding a title page and binding the pages together with a cover.

Color Poems . . . . Writing Poems

NAME a color. **HAVE** the children make up short sentences about the color, beginning each with the color itself. The lines can define (Red is hot!), describe (Red is Sarah's mittens), share a feeling (Red is pretty), and so on. **BEGIN** and **END** the group of lines with the color word (Red), and you will have a list poem. Children can write their own color poems at another time.

Poem Building . . . . Writing Poems

COPY the poem about snow (page 77) or some other favorite poem onto chart paper. Also **COPY** each line onto a separate sentence strip. After reciting the poem together a number of times, **DISTRIBUTE** the sentence strips and ask the children to build the poem line for line. Then **ASK** children to write their own lines to add to the poem. You may also **WRITE** a list poem about another topic, as a group.

ABC Poems . . . . Writing Poems

READ a variety of alphabet books to your class. Then, using the blackline master "ABC Poem" (Program Guide, "Forms of Writing" section, page 80), **HAVE** children choose a topic and write a list poem. **ENCOURAGE** them to decorate the page.

Going on a Picnic . . . . **Writing with Patterns**

GATHER children together in a circle. **INTRODUCE** the picnic game by reading and writing this line on the chalkboard: "I'm going on a picnic, and I'm bringing <u>pickles</u>." Going around the circle, **ASK** each child to repeat the line and all the foods named previously, ending with an additional food.

To establish some word patterns, ask for "p" words first (*pickles, pie, pudding,* etc.). When the "p" words are exhausted, start again with some other pattern (all "c" words, fruit words, vegetable words, etc.).

I'm one of many. . . . . **Writing with Patterns**

READ "I'm One of Three" by Angela Johnson. **USE** it as a model for a class book, "I'm One of Many." **ASK** each child to write and illustrate one page using this pattern: "I'm one of many who likes _____. I also like _____." **PUT** the pages together into a class book.

Patterns in Words . . . . **Writing with Patterns**

WRITE the words *can, pan, man* on the chalkboard. **ASK** children to find the pattern (each word ends in "an" and rhymes) and then volunteer more words for the list. Then write *cake, bake, shake* (or *big, bug, bib*) and continue the activity. **ASSIGN** the blackline master "Word Patterns" (Program Guide, "Forms of Writing" section, page 86), which involves children in a similar sorting activity.

Reading and Word Study

Context Clues .... **Reading New Words**

REMIND children that new words have other words around them, and sometimes pictures, to help them figure out the unknown words. **USE** the word *peppermint* on page 53 in the handbook as an example of an unknown word. **READ** the first sentence about Grandma, and the words "She smells like . . . "

Then **SAY** something like this: "I see the word begins with *p*, ends with *t*, and I know it's about a smell. I also see the word *pep* at the beginning. And the picture shows little red and white candies. The word must be *peppermint*!"

Word Parts .... **Reading New Words**

USE the following sentence from page 52 in the handbook as an example of reading a new word by looking for its parts.

It has a sunroof.

DEMONSTRATE reading a new word by finding the word parts in *sunroof*. Because it is a compound word, it will be easy to demonstrate this strategy. **BRAINSTORM** and **LIST** other compound words.

Listen for sounds. .... **Reading New Words**

WRITE the following words on the chalkboard:

seats   tan   dad   lot   like

TELL children that they can sound these words out. **TALK ABOUT** each word, defining it as a short- or long-vowel word. Then **SAY** each word slowly, listening for the beginning, middle, and end sounds. **HELP** children discover rhyming words for the listed words. **POINT OUT** that rhyming is a way to learn new words.

Show Me . . . . **Using Everyday Words**

ASK children to open their books to page 86 for a game. **BEGIN** the game by saying, "I'm thinking of a word that begins with *e* and ends with *t*." **HAVE** children write the word on little chalkboards or on slips of paper. **TELL** them to hold their words up when you say, "Show me." **ASK** for volunteers to use the word in a sentence. **CONTINUE** with other listed words. **ENCOURAGE** children to play "Show Me" (during their free time) with partners and in small groups.

Opposites . . . . **Using Everyday Words**

WRITE the following everyday words on the chalkboard:

after   come   big   man   new   take   down

ASK the children to open their books to "Using Everyday Words" beginning on page 86. **EXPLAIN** what "opposite" means, using *after* and *before* as examples. Then **HAVE** children find the opposites for the rest of the words. **WRITE** them on the board as the children find them. As a follow-up, **ASK** the children to use one pair of opposites in a sentence.

Ate/Eight . . . . **Using the Right Word**

WRITE the following sentences on the chalkboard:

1. She _____ the brownie.
2. The sum of 4 + 4 is _____ .
3. There are _____ boys in my class.
4. The dog _____ his bone.

ASK the children to choose *ate* or *eight* for each blank.
Then **HAVE** each child copy and illustrate two of the sentences.

For/Four . . . . **Using the Right Word**

WRITE the following sentences on the chalkboard:

1. This book is _____ you.
2. I saw _____ bears at the zoo.
3. She has _____ cats at her house.
4. This money is _____ my lunch.

ASK the children to choose *for* or *four* for each blank.
Then **HAVE** each child copy and illustrate two of the sentences.

Hunt and List . . . . Consonant Blends

DIVIDE the class into teams of four to six children. **RECALL** the definition of a blend (see handbook page 122). Then **GIVE** each team a long strip of paper. **INVITE** them to hunt for and list all the words they can find that begin with blends. (You may want to guide them to books and areas where words are readily available.) After hunting and listing, **MEET** to make a class list of blends.

Digraph Steps . . . . Consonant Digraphs

DRAW a large ladder or series of steps on the board with the digraphs "sh," "wh," "ch," and "th" on them. **HAVE** children take turns saying and writing words for the digraphs on each step.

Go fishing. . . . . Short Vowels

DRAW eight simple outlines of fish on the chalkboard. **WRITE** one short-vowel word on each fish. **ASK** volunteers to name the word on the fish, and then erase the whole thing with a "fishing pole," the eraser. At another time, this game may be played as a small-group activity. Children may use handbook page 124 as a starter.

New Words . . . . Long Vowels

WRITE these short-vowel words on the chalkboard:

can   cap   cut   Tim   rod

HAVE children say the words and dictate a sentence using each of them. (Write the sentences on the chalkboard.) Next **ADD** a final "e" to each word. Then have students say the long-vowel words and dictate five more sentences. **DISCUSS** how the sound and the meaning completely change for these words, just by adding an "e."

If you know . . . . Rhyming Families

READ pages 126-127. Then **ASK** children to complete the following sentence with as many rhyming words as they can: "If you know *cat*, you can read and write _____ ." **WRITE** the words on the board as they say and spell them. Then **HAVE** children break into small groups. **GIVE** each group three short- or long-vowel words and have them play "If you know . . ." as a rhyming game.

Let's read. . . . . Contractions

WRITE the following sentences on the board. Then **READ** them.

> It's time for bed.
>
> I'm not tired.
>
> We'll read a book.
>
> Let's read poems.
>
> I'll get the funny ones.

REWRITE the sentences using the two words instead of the contractions. **DISCUSS** with the children their feelings about which version sounds better to them. Then **TALK** about some of the differences between oral and written language.

1 + 1 = 1 . . . . Compound Words

COMPILE a list of compound words and then **WRITE** each of the shorter component words on large index cards. (**USE** page 129 of the handbook to get started.) **ATTACH** yarn so students can wear the cards around their necks and sit in a circle. One student stands and reads his or her word; then the classmate with a word that makes a compound word also stands. The class reads the two words to determine if they can be combined into a compound word. (Several students may have possible matches that make different compound words.)

The Student Almanac

Get in order. **Calendar Words**

MAKE flash cards of the months and the days. **GIVE** each child a card. **TELL** the children with the names of the days to stand in the back of the room, and those with the names of the months to stand in the front of the room. Then **HAVE** the "months" and "days" put themselves in order, beginning with Sunday and January. (Check the order against handbook page 133.)

Holiday Fun . . . . **Calendar Words**

ASK children to find their birthday months on page 133. Then **WRITE** a list of holidays on the chalkboard—ones that you will be celebrating during the school year. **LET** volunteers write the month next to each holiday. Then **HAVE** the children draw pictures about their birthdays or favorite holidays and label them with the appropriate month names.

Busy Days . . . . **Calendar Words**

DIVIDE the class into seven groups. **GIVE** each group a large sheet of paper with a day of the week written at the top. **ASK** the children to think of things they do on their given day. **APPOINT** one person in the group to write the activities on the paper, or **HAVE** each child write his or her own ideas. Later, **HAVE** the groups share their lists.

Crossword . . . . **Calendar Words**

WRITE the following pattern on the board. **ASK** children to fill it in using all the days of the week.

Days of the Week!

```
        _ _ e _ _ _ _ _
   _ _ _ _ _ d _ _ _
        _ _ n _ _ _ _
       _ e _ _ _ _ _ _ _
         s e v e n
   _ _ _ _ _ d _ _
     _ _ _ _ a _
     _ _ _ _ _ y
```

Color Touch .... **Colors**

NAME a color or **HOLD UP** a flash card of a color word. **ASK** for volunteers to go to a place in the classroom where they can touch something of that color. **CONTINUE** through all the color words, getting everyone involved in the activity.

Color and Number Walk .... **Colors**

TAKE children for a walk in the neighborhood. **HOLD** up a color word and ask children to count the things they see that are that color. Then change colors and repeat. When you get back to the classroom, **DISCUSS** the experience. (During the walk, older students or parents could record the colors and items for the children.)

Color Comparisons .... **Colors**

BEGIN by looking at pages 134-135 in the handbook and making comparisons like the following: as red as a ladybug, as green as a caterpillar, as purple as a tulip, and so on. Then **ASK** children to make comparisons with things that aren't on the page (as red as an apple). Hopefully these phrases will begin showing up in conversations and in writing.

Three-Way Match .... **Numbers**

MAKE UP three sets of flash cards—numbers from 0-10, number words from zero-ten, and patterns of dots from 0-10. **HAND OUT** the cards, and **DIRECT** children to find their matches (2/two/• •) and line up in the front of the room. (Giving clear directions for lining up will facilitate this three-way match. You may want to do only one number at a time, for instance.)

Season Graphs . . . . **Seasons and Weather**

TURN to page 136 of the handbook and **TALK** about the four seasons of the year. (If possible, have pictures of the season changes in your climate available.) Then **READ** and **EXPLAIN** the graph about favorite seasons on page 156 of the handbook. As a follow-up, **CREATE** your own classroom graph about the seasons.

Weather Symbols . . . . **Seasons and Weather**

Using the words and symbols on page 137, **TELL** children they can create their own symbols, too. **GIVE** them time to think about this and produce symbols. **DISPLAY** these somewhere in the classroom.

I'm going . . . . **Places**

PLAY the game "I'm Going." **MAKE UP** descriptive sentences like "I'm going to a place where many trees grow." **MODEL** three or four of these, with children finding the answers on pages 138-139. **INVITE** students to make up their own "I'm going . . . " sentences and play the game in small groups.

About This Place . . . . **Places**

ASK children to **MAKE UP** stories about the different places on pages 138-139. **TELL** them to "walk into one of the places" and imagine a story about it. **HAVE** them tell how the place looks, who is living or working in the place, what things are happening there, and so on. (At another time, children could write their stories.)

Root Work . . . . **Plants**

NOTE the roots of the flowers and the tree on pages 140-141 and **READ** what the rabbit is saying. To **DEMONSTRATE** that "roots take in water and food from the soil," **DO** the following experiment with the class. **CUT** a fresh end from two stalks of celery. **PUT** one stalk into an empty cup and the other into a cup of water with food coloring added. **OBSERVE** each of the stalks and record what happens over a period of 10 days. (This is a good learning-log project—see "Writing in Learning Logs" on pages 68-69 of the handbook.)

Label it. . . . . **Plants**

READ about the parts of plants on pages 140-141. **HELP** the children **PLAN** their own presentations of flowers or trees. They can do drawings, collages, paintings, or use real flowers if possible. They can also work alone, in pairs, or in small groups. The collection of work produced could be displayed as a decorative, informative bulletin board.

Bravo, Bread! . . . . **Food Pyramid**

READ about the food pyramid on pages 142-143. **ASK** children to tell you what they know about the importance of breads and grains in their diets. Also invite their questions. Then **DISCUSS** the placement of all of the other food groups. **ASK** them if they know why we should eat fewer foods from the top. As a follow-up, **HAVE** them draw a food pyramid and write names of foods that they like in each of the sections.

Healthy Hints . . . . **Food Pyramid**

CREATE a large poster or bulletin board of the food pyramid using markers, paints, or yarn for the outline. **INTRODUCE** the project to the children, recalling the value of knowing about the food pyramid. Over a period of time, **HAVE** the children fill the spaces with food pictures from magazines and grocery advertisements and with original art. **ENHANCE** the project with a fitting title and various captions.

Animal Poems . . . . **Animals**

INVOLVE children in writing a list poem or a cinquain about an animal they are studying. Then **HAVE** them write their own poems, possibly mounting them on construction-paper shapes of their animals. **REFER** children to "Writing Poems," pages 74-77 in the handbook, for help with this activity.

Visit my world. . . . . **Animals**

PRESENT an overview of pages 144-145. **Read** the name of the first habitat and write it on the chalkboard. Then **HAVE** the children name the animals in the picture that belong in that habitat. (**LIST** them.) **INVITE** volunteers to describe the place as though they were one of the animals that live there. **TRY** another habitat.

Animal Reports . . . . **Animals**

MAKE UP questions about different animals. Then **HAVE** children find the answers to these questions in their science and reading materials. Here are some sample questions:

What do _____ eat?   What sounds do _____ make?
Where do _____ live?   What can _____ do?

(The answers to these questions can become mini-reports.)

Sensational . . . . **Five Senses**

READ the poem on page 146. Then **LET** the students look at and discuss the pictures of the children and the sense that each represents (pages 146-147). **TALK** about how the senses work together.

Delicious Apples . . . . **Five Senses**

SLICE some apples and **PASS** a plate with a piece for each child. (Or give each child a whole apple.) **HAVE** children finish the following "sense sentences" with as many describing words as they can think of:

Apples look _____ .   Apples sound _____ .
Apples feel _____ .   Apples taste _____ .
Apples smell _____ .

Mapping the Playground . . . . **Using Maps**

TELL the children they will be making a map of their school play-ground. **ASK** them to notice where things are during recess. **SUPPLY** an outline of the playground on a large sheet of chart paper. **TALK** about how to place the compass rose. **DIVIDE** the class into groups to create symbols for various equipment and play areas. Afterward, **ASK** the children to share stories about games that are played in each area.

Going Places . . . . **Using Maps**

LIST six to eight famous places on the board: Statue of Liberty (N.Y.), St. Louis Gateway Arch (Mo.), Great Salt Lake (Utah), the Alamo (Tex.), Plymouth Rock (Mass.), Sears Tower (Ill.), Kennedy Space Center (Fla.), and the Golden Gate Bridge (Calif.). Using the map on page 149, **INVITE** children to find the states where these places are located. **ASK** them how many states they'd go through to get to their favorite destinations from where they live.

North, South, East, or West . . . . **Using Maps**

WRITE the following sentences on the chalkboard. **TELL** the children to use the maps on pages 150 and 151 to complete the statements. **REMIND** them to refer to the compass rose on each map. **INVITE** children to create their own fill-in-the-blank statements to share with each other.

1. The United States is _____ of Mexico.
2. Asia is _____ of Europe.
3. South America is _____ of Africa.
4. Australia is _____ of Asia.

On Time . . . . **Telling Time**

DRAW rectangles on the board or overhead. Think of times as dates. *New Years Day* is month *1* and day *1*. **WRITE** your birthday (month:day). (See handbook page 133 for a list of months.) Think of other fun times. **PLAY** "Digital Time" to prompt creative writing activities or storytelling.

| 1:01 | | : | | : | | : |

Seeing Patterns . . . . **Numbers 1 to 100**

ASK children to turn to the "Hundred Chart" on page 154. Read all the even numbers in unison. **TELL** the children this is also called counting by 2's. Then **DIRECT** half of the class to count together by 5's. Then **HAVE** the other half of the class count by 10's. **ASK** the children, "When do you use these counting skills?" (Possible answers: in games, telling time, counting money, reading maps and graphs, doing math problems, and so on)

Take your places! . . . . **Place Value**

DISCUSS place value using the chart on page 155. **EXPLAIN** that each place can have only one of these numbers: 0-9. **ASK** children what the largest possible number in the ones place would be (9). What is the largest possible number if you fill the ones place and the tens place? (99) What is the largest possible number if you fill all three places? (999)

Small Change . . . . **Money**

REFER children to page 157. **ASK** them which would be the greater amount of money: three dimes or five nickels, three quarters or one dollar, nine nickels or five dimes, and so on. **HAVE** them look at the "Hundred Chart" on page 154 if they need help counting by 5's and 10's.

Seven Ways to Make Six . . . . **Addition**

GIVE each child six counters. Instruct them to make two groups as pictured on page 158 in the handbook (a set of four and a set of two). **SHOW** how they can put these two groups together to make one new set of six. **ASK** them to put the counters into two different sets (3 + 3). Do they still have six? **CONTINUE** until they discover all the ways of making two groups that add up to six. **MAKE** minibooks in which each page illustrates one of the addition facts for six. **HAVE** them write out the addition sentence to go with each illustration. Minibooks for other addition facts could also be made. (Some children will discover three sets that make six: 2 + 2 + 2, 3 + 2 + 1, etc.)

A Piece of the Pie . . . . **Fractions**

DRAW two simple shapes on the chalkboard—a square and a circle. **INVITE** a volunteer to draw one line that will cut the figure into two equal pieces. **REFER** to page 159 in the handbook to talk about fractions. Have the child label each half ($\frac{1}{2}$). Next, ask a volunteer to draw another line that will divide the square and the circle into four equal pieces. Have them relabel these smaller pieces ($\frac{1}{4}$).

As a challenge, **DRAW** an equilateral triangle on the chalkboard. Have a child draw a line to cut the triangle into two equal pieces. Label it. Then **DRAW** another triangle and **ASK** if someone can draw lines to divide the triangle into three equal pieces. See the circle on page 159 ($\frac{1}{3}$) for a clue.

Who's next door? . . . . **Practicing Handwriting**

Who are the other first-grade teachers? **SEND** two "reporters" to the other teachers' doors to carefully copy the correct spelling of the other teachers' names. **HAVE** them report back to the class. **WRITE** the names on the chalkboard and **ASK** everyone to practice their handwriting by listing the first-grade teachers at your school, paying close attention to the capitals and periods in the titles.

Caption Writing . . . . **Practicing Handwriting**

POST a picture or **HAVE** students look at the photos and captions on page 56 of the handbook. **ASK** students to make up their own captions. When they are finished, **CHECK** for spelling, capitalization, and punctuation. Then **ASK** them to rewrite the captions on lined strips in their best handwriting. (This is one way to introduce the proofreading/editing/publishing process to young writers.)

Handbook MINILESSONS
Answer Key

This section provides an answer key for the few minilessons requiring specific answers. In most cases, the students' answers for the minilessons will vary.

The Process of Writing

Happy Birthday! (page 61)

Is today your birthday**?**   Wow, I love presents**!**

Yes**!** or (**.**)   How old are you**?**

This present is for you**.**   I'm seven years old**.**

Color the capital. (page 61)

My kitten is funny.   **T**he dog's name is **M**oppy.

Do you like him?   **S**he lives in **F**lorida.

Billy and **T**y have a dog.

Just One More (page 62)

kites	**keys**	**kings**	**kitchens**
kangaroos	**kids**	**kisses**	**kittens**

Holiday Marks (page 62)

Thanksgiving comes in the fall**.**   I love Thanksgiving Day**!**

What are you thankful for**?**   What holiday do you like**?**

Questions and Answers (page 62)

Where is Vito**?** —————— He's reading a joke book**.**

Do you see him**?** —————— He's in the yard**.**

Why is he laughing**?** —————— No, I don't**.** or (**!**)

Who is it? (page 64)

<u>me</u> = **Mom**   <u>I</u> = **Jake**   <u>He</u> = **Kaz**   <u>Her</u> = **Shavon**

Reading and Word Study

Opposites (page 76)

after – **before**	big – **little**	new – **old**	down – **up**
come – **go**	man – **woman**	take – **give**	

Ate/Eight (page 76)

1. **ate**   2. **eight**   3. **eight**   4. **ate**

For/Four (page 76)

1. **for**   2. **four**   3. **four**   4. **for**

The Student Almanac

Crossword (page 79)

Days of the <u>W</u>eek!

<u>T</u> <u>u</u> <u>e</u> s <u>d</u> <u>a</u> <u>y</u>
<u>S</u> <u>a</u> <u>t</u> <u>u</u> <u>r</u> d <u>a</u> y
<u>M</u> <u>o</u> n d <u>a</u> y
<u>W</u> <u>e</u> <u>d</u> <u>n</u> <u>e</u> <u>s</u> <u>d</u> <u>a</u> y
s <u>e</u> <u>v</u> <u>e</u> n
<u>T</u> <u>h</u> <u>u</u> <u>r</u> <u>s</u> d <u>a</u> y
<u>F</u> <u>r</u> <u>i</u> d a <u>y</u>
<u>S</u> <u>u</u> <u>n</u> <u>d</u> <u>a</u> y

North, South, East, or West (page 84)

1. **North**   2. **East**   3. **West**   4. **South**

Small Change (page 85)

Three dimes is a greater amount of money than five nickels.

One dollar is a greater amount of money than three quarters.

Five dimes is a greater amount of money than nine nickels.

Seven Ways to Make Six (page 85)

1. **4 + 2 = 6**   4. **1 + 5 = 6**   7. **6 + 0 = 6**
2. **2 + 4 = 6**   5. **5 + 1 = 6**
3. **3 + 3 = 6**   6. **0 + 6 = 6**

A Piece of the Pie (page 86)

 or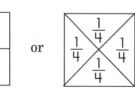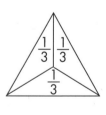

Evaluating/Assessing
MONITORING

The information in this section will help you evaluate your students' work. Included are general assessment guidelines, specific strategies for evaluating writing, and blackline masters of tips and guidelines that students can use as they respond to their own and others' writing.

Evaluating Your Students' Work

The ultimate goal of evaluation should be to help students improve their overall language proficiency. The guidelines and strategies that follow have been designed with these important points in mind.

Special Note: To help students become active participants in the evaluation process, make sure that they become acquainted with all four sections of *Write One*.

How should I evaluate my students?

The best methods of evaluation are those that address the process of learning as much as (or more than) the end products of learning. Evaluation should be . . .

— based on overall performance,
— interesting and functional in design,
— open-ended and flexible in scope, and
— meaningful and relevant to the particular learner.

In other words, the evaluation of students' work should be as *authentic* as possible.

What is meant by authentic assessment?

Authentic assessment is based on the principle that evaluation guides instruction. Authentic assessment is carried out through observations, interactions, and analysis.

— When you *observe* a student at work, notice his or her enthusiasm, diligence, care, creativity, neatness, and so on.
— When you *interact* with students, informally discuss their work in progress. Also engage in small-group discussions and conduct student-teacher conferences on a regular basis.
— When you *analyze* students' work, carefully examine their finished products. Highlight particular strengths, make suggestions for upcoming assignments, note your overall impressions, and give a mark or comment.

Should I use all three evaluation methods on each activity?

No, it would be next to impossible to observe and interact with students as well as analyze their work for each and every activity. However, we do encourage you to make use of all three methods of assessment throughout the course of the school year.

How should I evaluate writing?

A great deal has been written about the teaching of writing, including how to evaluate writing as a process rather than an end product. We have encapsulated much of this information, starting on page 97 of this section. Insights into assessing writing in progress (formative evaluation) as well as insights into assessing the end result of writing (summative evaluation) are addressed on these pages.

Recently, much attention has been given to special writing portfolios in which students demonstrate their best writing for evaluation at the end of a grading period. Portfolios place a significant part of the assessment process in the hands of the student writers because they can select and choose what they want evaluated. Students appreciate the sense of ownership this gives them. Teachers appreciate portfolios because the evaluation process can be used to assess a representative sample of students' products, as opposed to grading every written selection. (Guidelines for using writing portfolios are included in this section, starting on page 101.)

How should I address basic skills?

It has been demonstrated in study after study that learning the basic skills of grammar and punctuation out of context has little relevance for young learners and little carryover to their authentic language experiences. Students learn about their language as they use it in their daily lives and as they read, write, speak, listen, and think.

When you notice that a student has difficulty with a particular skill, help him or her learn from this problem. There's little incentive to learn if a student is penalized for making particular errors in an individual piece of writing. There's all the incentive in the world to learn if a student is rewarded for attempting to correct the error. **Always remember that evaluation guides instruction.**

Helping Each Student: If a student writer doesn't remember to use end punctuation marks, you can do a number of things:
— First note the error, showing the student why it is incorrect.
— Then refer the student to the handbook to learn how to correct the error.
— Model for the student "how to" correct the error.

Helping a Small Group: If you feel the error is common to many students in the class, consider assigning a related activity from the workshops or minilessons in the program. Let students know that you expect them to look for the problem in future writing assignments. Then, when you or a team evaluate their work at the end of the term, check to see what progress they are making.

What about handwriting?

Always remember that handwriting (manuscript and cursive) is not an end in itself. Students use handwriting to express themselves on paper. The main focus of evaluation should be to encourage and help students print and/or write more legibly and fluently over the long term. Students can evaluate their handwriting in final drafts using the handwriting hints and models on pages 162-164 in the *Write One* handbook.

Should I do all of the evaluating?

No, evaluation should be part of the learning process and should involve students as much as possible. Students automatically become involved in the process if they complete self-evaluation sheets or briefly reflect on their learning progress in a notebook or journal. Questions students might ask of themselves include the following: *What did I like about my writing? What was hard for me? What could I do to make my writing better next time?*

Students may also participate in peer-response groups. This works best if students have a predetermined checklist or guide with which to respond to their peer's work. (See the blackline master "Peer Conference" at the end of this section for a conferencing sheet.)

Special Note: Don't expect beginning writers to be careful, insightful, and fair evaluators right from the start. This skill will come only with practice, first modeled and then guided by the teacher.

Parents should also be involved in the evaluation process. For example, they can be encouraged to react (via written messages or in conferences) to their child's work, whether it be a series of daily assignments or a more important writing selection. Parents can also react to their child's portfolio at the end of a grading period. Ideally this should be done in a three-way parent-teacher-child conference.

Should I assign a grade or mark for each activity?

We certainly don't recommend it. Grading each activity is not a productive method of evaluating. Grades can hinder learning because they represent a stopping point, an end result. A more open-ended system of evaluation is much more in line with current research of best writing-instruction practices.

We believe that a basic "performance" score is sufficient for most of the writing activities. Teachers, with input from students, can assign students a predetermined number of points, a comment, or a mark upon completion of their work. (The score students receive depends on their basic performance.) We also believe teachers should make at least one specific, positive comment on individual activity sheets.

How should I grade or mark work at the end of a term?

If your students keep folders of their work and evaluations, including drafts and revisions, you have a complete collection or sampling for each student. You may also have students showcase their best work in a portfolio. If you noted observations and interactions during various activities, you have your own personal comments and reactions to consider. With the materials you have collected, there will be enough information to assess each student's performance.

Quarter or semester grading ought to reflect a measurement of each student's progress as a language learner—as much as, or even more than, the quality of the end products.

Evaluating Writing: A Closer Look

Several kinds of evaluation interest teachers today. **Formative evaluation** (evaluating while the students are developing their writing) and **summative evaluation** (evaluating the outcome of the students' efforts) are two of these evaluation types. Formative evaluation does not result in a grade or mark; summative evaluation usually does.

Formative Evaluation

Formative evaluation is most often used for prewriting activities, writing in progress, journal entries, and so forth. Three types of formative evaluation at the elementary level are widely used: the individual conference, the small-group conference, and peer conferencing.

The Individual Conference

The individual conference can occur informally at the student's desk or it can take place at a scheduled time. In the early stages of the writing process, responses and questions should be about writing ideas and procedures. Questions should be open-ended and the process should be positive. This gives the child "space" to talk—when a writer is talking, he or she is often thinking and planning. Teachers don't have to solve all writing problems for their students, but they can ask questions and suggest possible solutions.

In the editing and proofreading stage, a teacher might ask, "Why do you need a period here?" Students should try to answer the questions and add the correct punctuation marks when they can. With the inexperienced writer, it's best to limit the number of errors. Simply draw a double line to indicate where you stopped editing or proofreading the student's work. An individual conference can also be student directed if he or she finishes a draft, identifies a problem, or wants to share a revision or an improvement of some type.

"Teachers need to look at each individual writer, and what's more, each writer will demonstrate different writing behaviors with different writing tasks."

— Jo-Ann Parry and David Hornsby
Write On: A Conference Approach to Writing

The Small-Group Conference

The small-group conference may consist of groups of three to five students who are at various stages in the writing process or who are involved in the same type of writing project. The twofold goal of a small-group conference is to help students improve their own writing while also giving input to others. Minilessons work well in small-group conferences.

Consider holding a publisher's meeting during small-group conferences so students can help one another select writing to be published. Your role is to help students reach informed conclusions about their writing.

Peer Conferencing

Students may also learn how to conference with others (with minimal help from the teacher). We suggest that teachers always model the conferencing process before they ask young writers to work on their own. This may be done by modeling a peer conference in a role-playing situation with the class or in small-group situations where the teacher conferences with one student and the others watch and listen. When they are on their own, we find that young students work best in pairs, using some type of guide or checklist when they conference. The blackline master "Peer Conference" on page 103 of this section may work well for the children.

Summative Evaluation

Students need to understand and value the writing process as much as the final product. Their focus should be on personal goals, not grades. However, grades may be given to some of their completed work. This is when summative evaluation is important. The following general principles will help you evaluate finished written products:

1. Clearly establish the criteria for evaluating each written selection. Limit the criteria so you do not overwhelm the students or yourself.

2. Ask students to help you develop the criteria. This can be done in individual conferences or with the entire class. Students readily accept and understand criteria they have helped develop.

3. Offer students ample opportunities for formative evaluation before giving their final products grades or marks. Remember that students deserve credit for the work they have done during the writing process.

4. Attend first to overall meaning, organization, and details during summative evaluation. Correctness and neatness are also important, but they are only part of the complete writing picture.

5. Involve your students in summative evaluation. You can do this by providing them with a form that helps them to identify the best parts of their writing and list the problems they encountered.

Approaches for Summative Evaluations

A **checklist** can provide clear and ready information for evaluating a final product. Checklists employ various descriptions for assessing specific writing skills on a continuum. A checklist provides clear and ready information for evaluating a final product.

Teachers of young children can use a checklist, such as the following, to rate the effectiveness of a piece of writing.

Writing Checklist	Beginning Understanding	Developing	Fluent
Writing focuses on a topic.			
Writing is well organized.			
Writing has a variety of word choices.			
Punctuation, spelling, and capitalization are correct.			

Observational notes provide information about a writer's progress. These notes about specific writing behaviors can be written on individual cards, on sticky notes, or any way that works for a teacher. They provide a context for evaluating final papers. (For observational notes, Carol Avery, the author of ... *And with a Light Touch*, uses a daily record sheet that has a block for each child's name.)

Portfolio grading gives students an opportunity to be involved in the evaluation process. (See the next two pages for more information about portfolio assessment.)

A **performance system** is a quick and simple method of evaluation. A performance system is based on how a student applies what is learned. If students complete a writing activity, and it meets the previously established level of acceptability, they receive the preestablished grade or points for completing the assignment.

Using Writing Portfolios

More and more, teachers are using portfolios as an important part of their writing programs. Will portfolios be beneficial for you? Will they help you and your students assess their writing? Read on to find out.

What is a classroom portfolio?

A classroom portfolio is a representative sampling of a student's writing for evaluation. It differs from the traditional writing folder that contains all of a student's work.

Why should I ask students to compile classroom portfolios?

Students are directly involved in the assessment process as they go about choosing which pieces to include in their portfolios. Compiling portfolios also encourages students to monitor their own writing progress. They learn firsthand that writing is an involved, recursive process of writing and rewriting.

Teachers can utilize any or all methods of assessment when portfolios are used, including self-evaluation, peer evaluation, and traditional scoring (including checklists).

How many writing samples should be included in a portfolio?

You and your students should make that decision. However, as a guide, ask your students to collect at least three pieces of writing in a portfolio each quarter. All drafts for each written selection should be included. Rather than recopy journal entries of any type, photocopies can be made. Usually, students are also required to include a reflective piece or self-critique sheet that assesses their writing progress. The blackline master "For My Portfolio" at the end of this section can be used for this purpose.

When do portfolios work best?

Students need blocks of class time to work on writing if they are going to produce effective portfolios. If portfolios are used correctly, beginning writers become practicing writers. Portfolios are excellent teaching tools for classrooms that incorporate writing workshops.

How can I help my students with their portfolio writing?

Provide your students with many opportunities to discuss their writing with each other. Make daily sharing time an important part of your class. Expect your students to evaluate their own writing and the writing of their peers—and help them to do so. Also be available to guide students when they need help with their writing. Finally, create a stimulating classroom environment that encourages students to immerse themselves in writing.

How do I evaluate a portfolio?

Base the evaluation on the goals you and your students established at the beginning of the grading period, looking to the portfolio pieces for evidence of the achieved goals. Many teachers develop a critique sheet for assessment that is based on the goals established by the class. (It's very important that students know how many writing products they should include in their portfolios, how their written work should be arranged in their portfolios, and how the portfolios will be assessed.)

Note: See page 104 in this section for a master that will help children reflect on their portfolio choices.

Things Pets Need

Pets need food and fresh water. Pets like to be loved. They need a place to sleep. Pets like to have fun.

by Krista

Peer Conference

Use this sheet for helping your classmates with their writing.

Writer's Name _____

The writing is about _____

_____

_____

I like the part about _____

_____

_____

Here's an idea for making the writing better:

_____

_____

_____

Name _____

For My Portfolio

Use this sheet to tell about the
writing you put in your portfolio.

Title _____

I like this writing because _____

_____

_____

_____

When I was doing this writing, I learned _____

_____

_____

_____

Teacher's Name _____ Date _____

Reading-Writing
CONNECTION

In this section, you will find lists of important, high-interest titles that relate to many chapters in *Write One*. These lists will prove invaluable when planning units for these chapters.

Note: (C) = **Challenging**

Writing in Journals

Celia's Island Journal
by Celia Thaxter
(adapted by Loretta Kropinski), 1992

I Love Saturday
by Patricia Reilly Giff, 1989

Kitty: A Cat's Diary
by Robyn Supraner, 1986

Only Opal: The Diary of a Young Girl
by Jane Boulton, 1994

The 13th Clue
by Ann Jonas, 1992

Writing Friendly Notes and Letters

Armadillo from Amarillo
by Lynne Cherry, 1994

Arthur's Birthday
by Marc Brown, 1989

Days with Frog and Toad
by Arnold Lobel, 1979

Dear Mr. Blueberry
by Simon James, 1991

Dear Peter Rabbit/Querido Pedrin
by Alma Flor Ada, 1994

Don't Forget to Write
by Martina Selway, 1992

From Far Away
by Robert Munsch and Saoussan Askar, 1995

Here Comes the Mail
by Gloria Skurzynski, 1992

The Jolly Christmas Postman
by Janet Ahlberg, 1991

The Jolly Postman
by Janet and Allan Ahlberg, 1991

Little Bear's Friend
by Else Holmelund Minarik, 1960

A Village Full of Valentines
by James Stevenson, 1995

Writing Stories About Me

A Happy Day

One day baby Josh came home. He was in a yellow blanket. My mom let me hold him. He was blowing bubbles. He didn't cry.
by Jesse

Writing About Others

Abuela
by Arthur Dorros, 1991

Arthur's Family Vacation
by Marc Brown, 1993

Chester's Way
by Kevin Henkes, 1988

Daddy, Daddy Be There
by Candy Dawson Boyd, 1995

Dark Cloud Strong Breeze
by Susan Patron, 1994

Flower Garden
by Eve Bunting, 1994

Grandaddy's Place
by Helen V. Griffith, 1987

Grandma's Shoes
by Libby Hathorn, 1994

Grandpa and Bo
by Kevin Henkes, 1986

Julius, the Baby of the World Ⓒ
by Kevin Henkes, 1990

The Mother's Day Mice
by Eve Bunting, 1986

My Brother, Ant
by Betsy Byars, 1996

Our Granny
by Margaret Wild, 1994

Sam Is My Half-Brother
by Lizi Boyd, 1990

Snake Hunt
by Jill Kastner, 1993

Song and Dance Man Ⓒ
by Karen Ackerman, 1988

A Special Trade
by Sally Wittman, 1978

Taxi! Taxi!
by Carl Best, 1994

Tough Boris
by Mem Fox, 1994

A Visit to Gandma's
by Nancy Carlson, 1991

Writing a Description

BeBop-a-Do-Walk
by Sheila Hamanaka, 1995

Before the Storm
by Jane Yolen, 1995

Fish Eyes
by Lois Ehlert, 1990

**The 14 Forest Mice and
the Harvest Moon Walk**
by Kazuo Iwamura, 1991

**The 14 Forest Mice and
the Spring Meadow Picnic**
by Kazuo Iwamura, 1991

**The 14 Forest Mice and
the Summer Laundry Day**
by Kazuo Iwamura, 1991

**The 14 Forest Mice and
the Winter Sledding Day**
by Kazuo Iwamura, 1991

Funny Walks
by Judy Hindley, 1993

Ghost's Hour, Spook's Hour
by Eve Bunting, 1987

Indigo and Moonlight Gold
by Jan Spivey Gilchrist, 1993

In the Woods: Who's Been Here?
by Lindsey Barrett George, 1995

Mama Went Walking
by Christine Berry, 1990

One Hot Day
by Lynette Ruschak, 1994

Red Fox Running
by Eve Bunting, 1993

Thump, Thump, Rat-a-Tat-Tat
by Gene Baer, 1989

What Comes in Spring?
by Barbara Savadge Horton, 1992

Writing Directions

The Children's Step-by-Step
Cookbook
by Angela Wilkes, 1994

Froggy Learns to Swim
by Jonathan London, 1995

**From Pictures to Words:
A Book About Making a Book**
by Janet Stevens, 1995

How to Make an Apple Pie
and See the World
by Marjorie Priceman, 1994

The Paperboy
by Dav Pilkey, 1996

Tractor
by Craig Brown, 1995

Writing Captions

Cars! Cars! Cars!
by Grace Maccarone, 1995

Count and See
by Tana Hoban, 1972

The Creepy Thing
by Fernando Krahn, 1982

Going Ape Books (set)
by Bob Reese, 1983

Hop, Jump
by Ellen Stoll Walsh, 1993

Is It Red? Is It Yellow? Is It Blue?
by Tana Hoban, 1978

Joe Joe
by Mary Serfozo, 1993

My Five Senses
by Margaret Miller, 1994

Over, Under and Through and Other Spatial Concepts
by Tana Hoban, 1973

Push, Pull, Empty, Full
by Tana Hoban, 1972

See How I Grow
by Angela Wilkes, 1994

Sense Suspense: A Guessing Game for the Five Senses
by Bruce McMillan, 1994

Shadows and Reflections
by Tana Hoban, 1990

Shapes, Shapes, Shapes
by Tana Hoban, 1986

Stop-Go Fast-Slow
by Valjean McLenighan, 1982

A Time for Babies
by Ron Hirschi, 1993

What Food Is This?
by Rosmarie Hausherr, 1994

Where's My Cheese?
by Stan Mack, 1977

Zoom
by Isrvan Banyai, 1995

Butterflies move from place to place.

Writing Reports

Amazing World of Ants
by Francene Sabin, 1982

Backyard Insects
by Millicent E. Selsam and
Ron Goor, 1988

A Book About Your Skeleton
by Ruth B. Gross, 1994

Creepy, Crawly Caterpillars
by Margery Facklam, 1996

**A Day in the Life of a Baby Bear: The
Cub's First Swim**
by Peter and Susan Barrett, 1996

**Do They Scare You?
Creepy Creatures**
by Sneed B. Collard, 1993

First Grade Ladybugs
by Joanne Ryder, 1993

A First Look at Birds
by Millicent E. Selsam
and Joyce Hunt, 1973

Greg's Microscope
by Millicent E. Selsam, 1963

How Is a Crayon Made?
by Oz Charles, 1988

I Can Read About Baby Animals
by Elizabeth Warren, 1995

I Can Read About Horses
by Richard Harris, 1973

I Can Read About Spiders
by Deborah Merrians, 1977

Insects Are My Life
by Megan McDonald, 1995

Now I Know—Clouds
by Roy Wandelmaier, 1985

Now I Know—More About Dinosaurs
by David Cutts, 1982

Now I Know—What Is a Fish?
by David Eastman, 1982

The Popcorn Book
by Tomie dePaola, 1978

Puppies Are Special Friends
by Joanne Ryder, 1988

Storm
by W. Nikola-Lisa, 1993

The Storm Book
by Charlotte Zolotow, 1952

We Like Bugs
by Gladys Conklin, 1962

Wonders of the Forest
by Francene Sabin, 1982

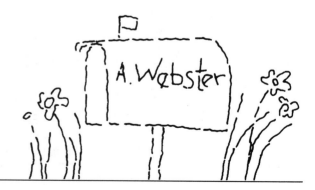

Making Alphabet Books

Alphabeast:
A Hide and Seek Alphabet Book
by Durga Bernhard, 1993

Alphabet City
by Stephen T. Johnson, 1995

Annie, Bea, and ChiChi Dolores:
A School Day Alphabet Book
by Donna Maurer, 1993

A You're Adorable
by Kaye, Buddy, Fred Wise
& Sidney Lippman, 1994

Chicka Chicka Boom Boom
by Bill Martin, Jr., 1989

City Seen from A to Z
by Rachel Isadora, 1983

Curious George Learns the Alphabet
by H. A. Rey, 1963

Dinosaur Alphabet Book
by Patricia Whitehead, 1985

Dr. Seuss's ABC
by Dr. Seuss, 1963

Eating the Alphabet
by Lois Ehlert, 1989

The Folks in the Valley:
A Pennsylvania Dutch ABC
by Jim Aylesworth, 1992

The Furry Alphabet Book
by Jerry Pallota, 1991

On Market Street
by Anita Lobel, 1981

Peter Rabbit's ABC
by Beatrix Potter, 1987

Pigs from A to Z
by Arthur Geisert, 1986

26 Letters and 99 Cents
by Tana Hoban, 1987

We Read: A to Z
by Donald Crews, 1967

Zooalphabets
by Robert Tallon, 1979

Words About Our School

A art   G gym
B bus   H heart
C calendar   I ice cream
D dancing   J jokes
E Eastview   K kindness
F friends   L lunch

Writing Poems

Dinosaur Dances
by Jane Yolen, 1990

**Doctor Knickerbocker
and Other Rhymes**
by David Booth, 1993

Dogs Don't Wear Sneakers
by Laura Numeroff, 1993

Dog Tales
by Janet McLean, 1995

Everyone Asked About You
by Theodore Faro Gross, 1990

Feathers for Lunch
by Lois Ehlert, 1990

A Frog Inside My Hat
compiled by Fay Robinson, 1993

Hailstones and Halibut Bones
by Mary O'Neil, 1961

**Hilary Knight's the Owl
and the Pussycat**
by Hilary Knight, 1983

In the Small, Small Pond
by Denise Fleming, 1993

In the Tall, Tall Grass
by Denise Fleming, 1991

**Is Somewhere Always Far Away?
Poems About Places**
by Leland B. Jacobs, 1993

Is Your Mama a Llama?
by Deborah Guarino, 1989

It's About Time!
selected by Lee Bennett Hopkins, 1993

**Mother Hubbard's Cupboard:
A Mother Goose Surprise Book**
by Laura Rader, 1993

My Son John
by Jim Aylesworth, 1994

**Never Take a Pig to Lunch and Other
Poems About the Fun of Eating**
selected by Nadine Bernard Westcott,
1994

"Not Now!" Said the Cow
by Joanne Oppenheim, 1989

Old Black Fly
by Jim Aylesworth, 1991

**Rata-Pata-Scata-Fata:
A Caribbean Story**
by Phillis Gershator, 1994

Sweet and Sour Animal Book
by Langston Hughes, 1994

Which Witch Is Which?
by Pat Hutchins, 1989

Whiskers and Rhymes
by Arnold Lobel, 1985

Who Can't Follow an Ant?
by Michael J. Pellowski, 1986

Writing with Patterns

Brown Bear, Brown Bear, What Do You See?
by Bill Martin, Jr., 1983

Can I Have a Stegasaurus, Mom? Can I? Please!?
by Lois G. Grambling, 1994

The Doorbell Rang
by Pat Hutchins, 1986

Drummer Hoff
by Barbara Emberley, 1967

The Elephant and the Bad Baby
by Elfrida Vipont, 1986

Everyone Asked About You
by Theodore Faro Gross, 1990

Five Ugly Monsters
by Tedd Arnold, 1995

Goodnight Moon
by Margaret Wise Brown, 1947

The Grouchy Ladybug
by Eric Carle, 1977

How Do You Say It Today, Jesse Bear?
by Nancy White Carlstrom, 1992

If Anything Ever Goes Wrong at the Zoo
by Mary Jean Hendrick, 1993

Is Your Mama a Llama?
by Deborah Guarino, 1989

It Could Always Be Worse
by Margot Zemach, 1976

I Was Walking down the Road
by Sarah E. Barchas, 1993

Jump, Frog, Jump!
by Robert Kalan, 1981

King of the Dinosaurs: Tyrannosaurus Rex (C)
by Michael Berenstain, 1989

The Little Engine That Could
by Watty Piper, 1976

Mary Wore Her Red Dress
by Merle Peek, 1985

The Mitten
by Jan Brett, 1989

More Spaghetti, I Say!
by Rita Golden Gelman, 1992

Mother Halverson's New Cat
by Jim Aylesworth, 1989

No Jumping on the Bed
by Tedd Arnold, 1987

No More Water in the Tub!
by Tedd Arnold, 1995

Writing with Patterns (continued)

Polar Bear, Polar Bear, What Do You Hear?
by Bill Martin, Jr., 1991

Skyfire
by Frank Asch, 1984

This Is the Bear
by Sarah Hayes, 1986

This Is the Bear and the Scary Night
by Sarah Hayes, 1992

Three Billy Goats Gruff
by Ted Dewan, 1995

Time for Bed
by Mem Fox, 1993

Tough Boris
by Mem Fox, 1994

Trouble with Trolls
by Jan Brett, 1992

Where's the Baby?
by Pat Hutchins, 1988

Why Can't I Fly?
by Rita Golden Gelman, 1986

Using Theme Words

Calendar Words

All Year Long
by Nancy Tafuri, 1983

Bear Child's Book of Special Days
by Anne Rockwell, 1989

January Brings the Snow: A Book of Months
by Sara Coleridge, 1990

Mother Goose's Words of Wit and Wisdom: A Book of Months
by Tedd Arnold, 1990

Tuesday
by David Wiesner, 1991

When This Box Is Full
by Patricia Lillie, 1993

Using Theme Words (continued)

Numbers and Colors

Color Dance
by Ann Jonas, 1989

Color Farm
by Lois Ehlert, 1990

Color Zoo
by Lois Ehlert, 1989

Counting Cows
by Woody Jackson, 1995

Dirty Dozen Dizzy Dogs
by William Hooks, 1990

Frog Counts to Ten
by John Liebler, 1994

Gray Rabbit's 1, 2, 3
by Alan Baker, 1994

Little Blue and Little Yellow
by Leo Lionni, 1959

Mouse Paint
by Ellen Stoll Walsh, 1989

My Color Is Panda
by Deborah Winograd, 1993

Peter Rabbit's Colors
by Beatrix Potter, 1988

Red Bear
by Bodel Rikys, 1992

Red Day, Green Day
by Edith Kunhardt, 1992

Ten Flashing Fireflies
by Philemon Sturges, 1995

**Ten Tiny Turtles:
A Crazy Counting Book**
by Paul Cherrill, 1995

White Rabbit's Color Book
by Alan Baker, 1994

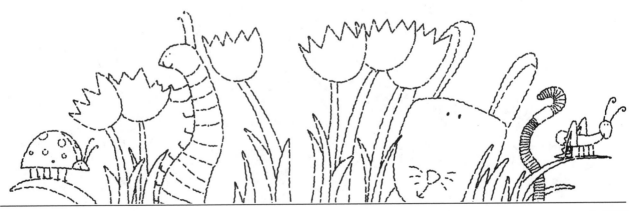

Using Theme Words (continued)

Seasons and Weather

How Does the Wind Walk?
by Nancy White Carlstrom, 1993

**Just Around the Corner:
Poems About the Seasons**
by Leland B. Jacobs, 1993

Outside, Inside
by Carolyn Crimi, 1995

Weather
selected by Lee Bennett Hopkins, 1994

The Winter Noisy Book
by Margaret Wise Brown, 1994

Plants

A Flower Grows
by Ken Robbins, 1990

Look at Leaves
by Rena K. Kirkpatrick, 1985

Look at Trees
by Rena K. Kirkpatrick, 1985

Plants Illustrated Series
published by Dorling, 1992

**Tree of Life: The World of
the African Baobab**
by Barbara Bash, 1989

Places

City Noise
by Karla Kuskin, 1994

Deserts
by Elsa Posell, 1982

First Look at Mountains
by Susan Baker, 1991

Lucy's Summer
by Donald Hall, 1995

My River
by Shari Halpern, 1992

The Summer Sands
by Sherry Garland, 1995

Food Pyramid

Bread Bread Bread
by Ann Morris, 1989

Let's Eat!
by True Kelley, 1989

Nutrition
by Leslie Jean LeMaster, 1985

Pierrot's ABC Garden
by Anita Lobel, 1993

Siggy's Spaghetti Works
by Peggy Thomson, 1993

What Food Is This?
by Rosmarie Hausherr, 1994

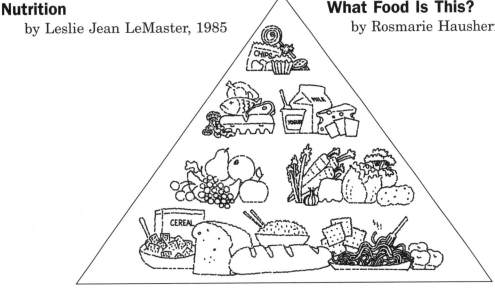

Animals of the . . .

African Animals ABC
by Philippa Alys-Browne, 1995

Animal Lingo
by Pam Conrad, 1995

Biggest, Strongest, Fastest
by Steve Jenkins, 1995

Fishy Facts
by Ivan Chermayeff, 1994

The Salamander Room
by Anne Mazer, 1991

Wild Animal Go-Round
by Mary Ling, 1995

Five Senses

Hearing
by J. M. Parramon and J. J. Puig, 1985

Look at Your Eyes
by Paul Showers, 1992

My Five Senses
by Margaret Miller, 1994

Smell
by J. M. Parramon and J. J. Puig, 1985

Taste
by J. M. Parramon and J. J. Puig, 1985

Touch
by J. M. Parramon and J. J. Puig, 1985

RESOURCES
for Teachers

The resources in this section are helpful titles teachers may consult for additional information related to each handbook section. There are also references that address "Evaluating/Assessing/Monitoring" and the "Reading-Writing Connection."

RESOURCES FOR TEACHERS

The **Process** of Writing

Avery, Carol. *. . . And with a Light Touch: Learning About Reading, Writing, and Teaching with First Graders*. Portsmouth: Heinemann, 1993.

Calkins, Lucy McCormick. *The Art of Teaching Writing*. Portsmouth: Heinemann, 1994.

Calkins, Lucy McCormick. *Living Between the Lines*. Portsmouth: Heinemann, 1991.

Crafton, Linda K. *Standards in Practice, Grades K-2*. Urbana, IL: NCTE, 1996.

Fairfax, Barbara, and Adela Garcia. *Read! Write! Publish! Making Books in the Classroom Grades 1-5*. Cypress, CA: Creative Teaching Press, 1992.

Fisher, Bobbi. *Inside the Classroom: Teaching Kindergarten and First Grade*. Portsmouth: Heinemann, 1996.

Fletcher, Ralph. *What a Writer Needs*. Portsmouth: Heinemann, 1993.

Gentry, J. Richard. *Spel . . . Is a Four-Letter Word*. Portsmouth: Heinemann, 1987.

Graves, Donald H. *A Fresh Look at Writing*. Portsmouth: Heinemann, 1994.

Harwayne, Shelley. *Lasting Impressions: Weaving Literature into the Writing Workshop*. Portsmouth: Heinemann, 1992.

Hydrick, Janie. *Parent's Guide to Literacy for the 21st Century*. Urbana, IL: NCTE, 1996.

Jensen, Julie M. "What Do We Know about the Writing of Elementary School Children?" *Language Arts* 70:4 (1993).

Johnson, Paul. *A Book of One's Own: Developing Literacy Through Making Books*. Portsmouth: Heinemann, 1992.

Kovacs, Deborah, and James Prowler. *Meet the Authors and Illustrators: 60 Creators of Favorite Children's Books Talk About Their Work*. New York: Scholastic, 1991.

Lensmire, Timothy J. *When Children Write*. New York: Teacher's College Press, 1994.

Moffett, James, and Betty Wagner. *Student-Centered Language Arts, K-12*. Portsmouth: Heinemann, 1992.

Murray, Donald. *Learning by Teaching*. Portsmouth: Boynton Cook, 1982.

Nathan, Ruth, et al. *Classroom Strategies That Work: An Elementary Teacher's Guide to Process Writing*. Portsmouth: Heinemann, 1989.

Petty, Walter T., Dorothy C. Petty, and Richard T. Salzer. "Supporting the Writing Process." In *Experiences in Language*. Boston: Allyn and Bacon, 1994.

Ross, Elinor Parry. *The Workshop Approach: A Framework for Literacy*. Norwood, MA: Christopher-Gordon, 1996.

Routman, Regie. *Invitations: Changing as Teachers and Learners, K-12*. Portsmouth: Heinemann, 1994.

Routman, Regie. *Literacy at the Crossroads*. Portsmouth: Heinemann, 1996.

Short, Kathy G., Jerome C. Harste, and Carolyn Burke. *Creating Classrooms for Authors and Inquirers*. Portsmouth: Heinemann, 1996.

Smith, Jennifer. "Periodicals That Publish Children's Original Work." *Language Arts* 65:2 (1988).

Tompkins, Gail E. *Teaching Writing*. New York: Macmillan College Publishing Company, 1993.

Wilde, Sandra. *You Kan Red This! Spelling and Punctuation for Whole Language Classrooms, K-6*. Portsmouth: Heinemann, 1992.

The **Forms** of Writing

Barchers, Suzanne I. *Creating and Managing the Literate Classroom*. Englewood, CO: Libraries Unlimited, 1990.

Barkin, Carol, and Elizabeth James. *Sincerely Yours: How to Write Great Letters*. New York: Clarion, 1993.

Bunting, Jane. *The Childen's Visual Dictionary*. London: Dorling Kindersley, 1995.

Chatton, Barbara. *Using Poetry Across the Curriculum: A Whole Language Approach*. Phoenix: Oryx Press, 1993.

Clark, Roy Peter. *Free to Write: A Journalist Teaches Young Writers*. Portsmouth: Heinemann, 1987.

Cullinan, Bernice, et al. *Three Voices: An Invitation to Poetry Across the Curriculum*. York, ME: Stenhouse, 1995.

D'Arcy, Pat. *Making Sense, Shaping Meaning*. Portsmouth: Heinemann, 1989.

Doris, Ellen. *Doing What Scientists Do: Children Learn to Investigate Their World*. Portsmouth: Heinemann, 1991.

Gamberg, R., et al. *Learning and Loving It: Theme Studies in the Classroom*. Portsmouth: Heinemann, 1988.

Glover, Mary Kenner. *Making School by Hand*. Urbana, IL: NCTE, 1995.

Graves, Donald. *Experiment with Fiction*. Portsmouth: Heinemann, 1989.

Hamilton, Martha, and Mitch Weiss. *Children Tell Stories*. Katonah, NY: Richard C. Owens, 1990.

Heard, Georgia. *For the Good of the Earth and the Sun: Teaching Poetry*. Portsmouth: Heinemann, 1989.

Janeczko, Paul. *Poetry from A to Z*. New York: Bradbury Press, 1994.

Johnson, Terry, and Daphne Louis. *Bringing It All Together: A Program for Literacy*. Portsmouth: Heinemann, 1990.

Kaye, Peggy. "Write a Letter." In *Games for Writing*. New York: Farrar, Straus & Giroux, 1995.

Kobrin, Beverly. *Eyeopeners II*. New York: Scholastic, 1995.

Lansky, Bruce, director. *Free Stuff for Kids, 1995*. Deephaven, MN: Meadowbrook, 1994.

Larrick, Nancy. *Let's Do a Poem! Introducing Poetry to Children*. New York: Delacorte Press, 1991.

Livingston, Myra Cohn. *Poem-Making: Ways to Begin Writing Poetry*. New York: Harper-Collins, 1991.

McIlwain, John. *The Dorling Kindersley Children's Illustrated Dictionary*. London: Dorling Kindersley, 1994.

Milz, Vera E. "Supporting Literacy Development: On the First Day in First Grade and Throughout the Year." In *Portraits of Whole Language Classrooms: Learning for All Ages*. Edited by Heidi Mills and Jean Anne Clyde. Portsmouth: Heinemann, 1990.

Moir, Hughes, Melissa Cain, and Leslie Prosak-Beres. *Collected Perspectives: Choosing and Using Books for the Classroom*. Boston: Christopher-Gordon, 1992.

Ohanian, Susan. "Across the Curriculum from A to Z." *Learning* 18:2 (1987).

Ohanian, Susan. *Who's in Charge? A Teacher Speaks Her Mind*. Portsmouth: Heinemann, 1994.

Oliver, Mary. *A Poetry Handbook*. New York: Harcourt Brace and Co., 1994.

Ostrow, Jull. *A Room with a Different View: First Through Third Graders Build Community and Create Curriculum*. York, ME: Stenhouse, 1995.

Robb, Laura. *Whole Language, Whole Learners: Creating a Literature-Centered Curriculum*. New York: Quill/William Morrow, 1995.

Scarry, Richard. *Richard Scarry's Best Word Book Ever*. New York: Golden Press, 1963.

Sorenson, Marilou, and Barbara Lehman. *Teaching with Children's Books*. Urbana, IL: NCTE, 1995.

Stevens, Carla. *A Book of Your Own: Keeping a Diary or Journal*. New York: Clarion Books, 1993.

Stillman, Peter. *Families Writing*. Cincinnati: Writer's Digest Books, 1989.

Ward, Geoff. *I've Got a Project On . . . .* Portsmouth: Heinemann, 1988.

Reading and Word Study

Allington, Richard L., and Patricia M. Cunningham. *Schools That Work: Where All Children Read and Write*. New York: HarperCollins, 1996.

Barchers, Suzanne I. *Teaching Language Arts: An Integrated Approach*. St. Paul, MN: West Publishing Co., 1994.

Bear, Donald, et al. *Words Their Way: Word Study for Phonics, Vocabulary, and Spelling Instruction*. Englewood Cliffs: Merrill/Prentice-Hall, 1995.

Brown, Hazel, and Brian Cambourne. *Read and Retell*. Portsmouth: Heinemann, 1990.

Cullinan, Bernice, ed. *Invitation to Read: More Children's Literature in the Reading Program*. Newark: International Reading Association, 1992.

Cunningham, Patricia. *Phonics They Use: Words for Reading and Writing*. 2nd ed. New York: HarperCollins, 1995.

Fountas, Irene C., and Gay S. Pinnell. *Guided Reading*. Portsmouth: Heinemann, 1996.

Green, Joseph. *The Word Wall: Teaching Vocabulary Through Immersion*. Portsmouth: Heinemann, 1993.

Mills, Heidi, Timothy O'Keefe, and Diane Stephens. *Looking Closely: Exploring the World of Phonics in One Whole Language Classroom*. Urbana, IL: NCTE, 1991.

Mooney, Margaret E. *Reading to, with, and by Children*. Katonah, NY: Richard C. Owen, 1990.

Norton, Donna, and Saundra E. Norton. *Language Arts Activities for Children*. New York: Merrill, 1994.

Peterson, Ralph, and Maryann Eeds. *Grand Conversations: Literature Groups in Action*. New York: Scholastic, 1990.

Powell, Debbie, and David Hornsby. *Learning Phonics and Spelling in a Whole Language Classroom*. New York: Scholastic, 1993.

Smith, Frank. *Reading Without Nonsense*. 3rd ed. New York: Teachers College Press, 1997.

Weaver, Constance. *Reading Process and Practice*. 2nd ed. Portsmouth: Heinemann, 1994.

Young, Sue. *The Rhyming Dictionary*. New York: Scholastic, 1994.

The Student **Almanac**

Baker, Ann, and Johnny Baker. *Mathematics in Process*. Portsmouth: Heinemann, 1990.

Buckley, Susan, and Elspeth Leacock. *Hands-On Geography*. New York: Scholastic, 1993.

Burns, Marilyn. *About Teaching Mathematics: A K-8 Resource*. New Rochelle: Math Solutions Publications, 1992.

Carlisle, Madelyn Wood. *Marvelously Meaningful Maps*. Hauppauge, NY: Barron's, 1992.

Chaille, Christine, and Lori Britain. *The Young Child as Scientist*. New York: HarperCollins, 1991.

Cyclopedia: The Portable Visual Encyclopedia. Philadelphia: Running Press, 1993.

Fisher, Bobbi. *Thinking and Learning Together: Curriculum and Community in a Primary Classroom*. Portsmouth: Heinemann, 1995.

Kanter, Patsy F., and Janet G. Gillespie. *Every Day Counts Calendar Math*. Wilmington, MA: Great Source, 1998.

Knowlton, Jack, and Harriet Barton. *Maps & Globes*. New York: HarperCollins, 1985.

Lipson, Marjorie Y., et al. "Integration and Thematics: Integration to Improve Teaching and Learning." *Language Arts* 70:4 (1993).

Losq, Christine. *Math Zones*. Wilmington, MA: Great Source, 1998.

Perham, Molly, and Philip Steele. *The Children's Illustrated World Atlas*. Philadelphia: Courage Books, 1992.

Pigdon, Keith, and Marilyn Wooley. *The Big Picture: Integrating Children's Learning*. Portsmouth: Heinemann, 1993.

Taylor, Barbara. *Maps and Mapping*. New York: Kingfisher Books, 1993.

Evaluating/Assessing/**Monitoring**

Allington, Richard L., and Patricia M. Cunningham. *Schools That Work*. New York: HarperCollins, 1996.

Anthony, Robert, et al. *Evaluating Literacy: A Perspective for Change*. Portsmouth: Heinemann, 1991.

Cambourne, Brian. *The Whole Story: Natural Learning and the Acquisition of Literacy in the Classroom*. New York: Scholastic, 1989.

Davies, Anne, et al. *Together Is Better: Collaborative Assessment, Evaluation, and Reporting*. Winnipeg: Pegis, 1992.

Graves, Donald H., and Bonnie S. Sunstein, eds. *Portfolio Portraits*. Portsmouth: Heinemann, 1992.

Harp, Bill, ed. *Assessment and Evaluation in Whole Language Programs*. Norwood, MA: Christopher-Gordon, 1991.

Jett-Simpson, Mary, and Lauren Leslie. *Ecological Assessment*. Schofield, WI: Wisconsin State Reading Association, 1994.

Myers, Miles, and Elizabeth Spalding. *Assessing Student Performance, Grades K-5*. Urbana, IL: NCTE, 1997.

Rhodes, Lynn K., ed. *Literacy Assessment: A Handbook of Instruments*. Portsmouth: Heinemann, 1993.

Rhodes, Lynn K., and Nancy Shanklin. *Windows into Literacy: Assessing Learners, K-8*. Portsmouth: Heinemann, 1993.

Woodward, Helen. *Negotiated Evaluation: Involving Children and Parents in the Process*. Portsmouth: Heinemann, 1994.

Reading-Writing **Connection**

Beaty, Janice J. *Picture Book Storytelling: Literature Activities for Young Children*. Fort Worth: Harcourt Brace, 1994.

Bishop, Rudine Sims, ed. *Kaleidoscope: A Multicultural Booklist for Grades K-8*. Urbana, IL: NCTE, 1994.

Cullinan, Bernice E. *Literature and the Child*. 2nd ed. San Diego: Harcourt Brace Jovanovich, 1989.

Danielson, Kathy Everts, and Jan LaBonty. *Integrating Reading and Writing Through Children's Literature*. Boston: Allyn and Bacon, 1993.

Gillespie, John T., and Corinne J. Naden, eds. *Best Books for Children: Preschool Through Grade 6*. 5th ed. New Providence, NJ: R. R. Bowker, 1994.

Hart-Hewins, Linda, and Jan Wells. *Real Books for Reading*. Portsmouth: Heinemann, 1990.

Hearne, Betsy. *Choosing Books for Children*. New York: Delacorte, 1990.

Jensen, Julie, and Nancy L. Roser, eds. *Adventuring with Books: A Booklist for Pre-K–Grade 6*. 10th ed. Urbana, IL: NCTE, 1993.

Kruse, Ginny Moore, and Kathleen T. Horning. *Multicultural Literature for Children and Young Adults*. 3rd ed. University of Wisconsin-Madison: Cooperative Children's Book Center, 1991.

Sharkey, Paulete Bochnig, and Jim Roginski, eds. *Newbery and Caldecott Medal and Honor Books in Other Media*. New York: Neal-Schuman Publishers, 1992.

Sutherland, Zena, and May Hill Arbuthnot. *Children and Books*. 8th ed. New York: HarperCollins, 1991.

Sutton, Wendy K., ed. *Adventuring with Books: A Booklist for Pre-K–Grade 6*. Urbana, IL: NCTE, 1997.

Program OVERVIEW

This overview helps answer a very important question: What is the **Write One Language Series** all about? Of special interest to you will be the introduction to the *Language Series,* the complete *Write One* program, on page 132. The program activities reflect the table of contents of the handbook. This overview concludes with explanations of the various program activities.

Introducing . . .

A Closer Look at . . .

The Complete *Write One* Program

There are four main components in the program: (1) the **Write One** student handbook, (2) the **Write One Teacher's Guide,** (3) the student **Buddy Book** of writing activities, and (4) the **Write One Language Series Program Guide.** Here's how the different components can work in your classroom:

1 The **Write One** student handbook can be used as a classroom resource for writing, thinking, and learning. The handbook serves as students' core resource.

2 The **Teacher's Guide** provides basic planning ideas, start-up activities, and minilessons to support the handbook.

3 The **Buddy Book** is a place for students to learn and to write. Its pages are linked to the *Write One* handbook. There are three sections: an ABC section for listing new words, a journal section for personal writing, and a special section for different kinds of writing the students can try.

4 The **Program Guide** (ring-binder format) provides everything you need to teach this comprehensive program including complete program planning guidelines, teacher's notes, and blackline masters that coordinate with the chapters in the *Write One* handbook. All *Program Guide* activities are reproducible.

Program Activities

The **Process** of Writing

All About Writing

Jenny Writes

Being a Writer

Steps in the Writing Process

Rules for Writing

Writing Sentences

Using Capital Letters

Making Plurals

Using Punctuation

Understanding Our Language

> Program activities include teacher's chapter notes, blackline masters, and minilessons—everything you need to build an active, engaging language program.

The **Forms** of Writing

Personal Writing

Writing in Journals

Writing Lists

Writing Friendly Notes

Writing Friendly Letters

Writing Stories About Me

Subject Writing

Writing About Others

Writing a Description

Writing Directions

Writing Captions

Writing About Books

Research Writing

Writing Reports

Making Alphabet Books

Writing in Learning Logs

Story and Poetry Writing

Writing Stories

Writing Poems

Writing with Patterns

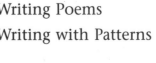

Reading and Word Study

Reading Skills

Reading to Understand
Reading New Words
Using Everyday Words
Using the Right Word

Word-Study Skills

Alphabet Sounds and Words
Consonant Blends
Consonant Digraphs
Short Vowels
Long Vowels
Rhyming Families
Contractions
Compound Words

The Student **Almanac**

Helpful Words, Maps, and Lists

Using Theme Words
Calendar Words
Numbers and Colors
Seasons and Weather
Places
Plants
Food Pyramid
Animals
Five Senses
Using Maps

Working with Math
Telling Time
Numbers 1 to 100
Place Value
Bar Graphs
Money
Addition and Subtraction
Fractions
Knowing About a Computer
Practicing Handwriting

A Closer Look at
Chapter Notes

These notes introduce you to chapters in *Write One* and provide implementation guidelines, planning notes, reproducible blackline masters, and minilessons.

Introductory Page ......⋯

Implementation Guidelines

Related Minilessons .⋯

Writing with Patterns

(handbook pages 78-79)

Stories and songs written with patterns of rhythm, repetition, and rhyme readily engage readers—and writers. Texts like "Brown Bear, Brown Bear" by Bill Martin, Jr., and "Down by the Bay" by Raffi encourage early success in reading, and are easily modeled by beginning writers. Pattern books and songs also encourage group participation and are lots of fun.

Rationale
✓ Pattern songs and stories engage early readers and writers.
✓ Children at all levels can recognize and imitate the patterns in stories, songs, and poems.

Major Concepts
✳ Children are able to identify the rhyme and beat in the songs and stories they hear, read, and write. (pages 78-79)
✳ After exposure to predictable texts, children can write their own. (page 79)

Planning Notes
Materials: Several types of pattern stories, chart paper, blackline masters, writing and drawing materials

Math Connections: There are many patterns and predictable outcomes in math. Children can find number patterns when they work with manipulatives and charts. Look at the hundred chart on page 154. Help the children discover the obvious patterns of 1's, 5's, and 10's. See if they can discover other patterns on their own.

Science Connections: The study of weather lends itself to finding and discussing patterns. Use pages 136-137 in the handbook to talk about the weather patterns of each season; the sky, wind, and air before and during rainstorms, snowstorms, or violent storms; lightning and thunder; and any other weather or seasonal patterns children have noticed.

Writing with Patterns 83

Minilessons for Writing with Patterns

Going on a Picnic . . . . **Writing with Patterns**

GATHER children together in a circle. **INTRODUCE** the picnic game by reading and writing this line on the chalkboard: "I'm going on a picnic, and I'm bringing <u>pickles</u>." Going around the circle, **ASK** each child to repeat the line and all the foods named by previous children, ending with an additional food of their own.
 To establish some word patterns, ask for "p" words first (*pickles, pie, pudding,* etc.). When the "p" words are exhausted, start again with some other pattern (all "c" words, fruit words, vegetable words, etc.).

I'm one of many. . . . . **Writing with Patterns**

READ "I'm One of Three" by Angela Johnson. **USE** it as a model for a class book, "I'm One of Many." **ASK** each child to write and illustrate one page using this pattern: "I'm one of many who likes _____. I also like _____."
PUT the pages together into a class book.

Patterns in Words . . . . **Writing with Patterns**

WRITE the words *can, pan, man* on the chalkboard. **ASK** children to find the pattern (each word ends in "an" and rhymes) and then volunteer more words for the list. Then write *cake, bake, shake* (or *big, bug, bib*) and continue the activity. **ASSIGN** the blackline master "Word Patterns," which involves children in a similar sorting activity.

Writing with Patterns 87

Write to the Handbook

Getting Started (handbook pages 78-79)
● Introduce "Writing with Patterns," pages 78-79. Read and sing "The Itsy Bitsy Spider" on page 78. Then read and sing the song about the lobster on page 79. Help children discover the rhythm and rhyme patterns that relate these two songs.
● Next, work with the children to write their own song, as a class, patterned after "The Itsy Bitsy Spider." (Take dictation on chart paper.) Help students choose a subject and start composing. Remember to keep the rhythm of the original song—as well as the rhyme pattern. Clap it out or sing it together to get the feel of the beat. Encourage children who want to write their own verses to do so.

Classroom Applications
Large Group
● Read aloud a version of "The Gingerbread Man." The patterns in the story include the repetition of the line "Run, run, as fast as you can. You can't catch me! I'm the Gingerbread Man!" and the accumulation of characters, one at a time. Call attention to the patterns, and the children will soon become aware of similar patterns in stories like "The Little Red Hen," "The Napping House" by Audrey Wood, "I'm One of Three" by Angela Johnson, and "Mrs. Wishy Washy" by Joy Cowley.
Small Group
● "The Gingerbread Man" is a perfect story to act out. Divide the children into small "troupes." Some groups may have one reader while the rest act. Some may be more creative, changing the characters and action of the story—creating their own dramatic versions.
Individual
● Many pattern stories have tightly structured text and adapt well to fill-in-the-blank activities. Patterns and stories like "Mary Wore Her Red Dress" help children create texts with ease. (There are various story and song versions of "Mary Wore Her Red Dress," including one by Merle Peek.) Using the blackline master "Jenny's Shirt" (adapted from "Mary Wore Her Red Dress"), have each student write his or her own verse for this song. When the pages are finished, make a class book.

84 *Writing with Patterns*

A Closer Look at
Blackline Masters

The type and number of masters vary from unit to unit. For example, the masters for "The Process of Writing" and "The Forms of Writing" address different stages in the development of students' writing, and the masters for "Reading and Word Study" relate to word-study skills practice.

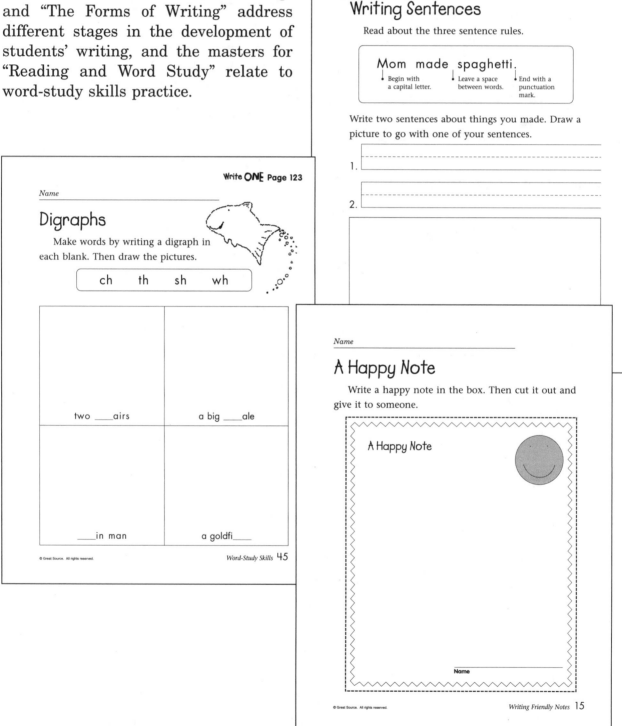

A Closer Look at
Minilessons

Minilessons are short, focused teaching opportunities that cover important writing or learning ideas from the handbook. Most minilessons can be completed in 15-20 minutes. They work especially well in a writing-workshop classroom. The minilessons in the "Getting Started" section of the *Program Guide* are models for the lessons you may wish to develop on your own as you use the handbook.

Start-Up Minilessons

▶ Conduct minilessons on a regular basis to give your students practice with *Write One*. Most minilessons can be completed in 15-20 minutes.

The Process of Writing

Directions are clearly stated. ···········▶

Sentence Sense . . . . **Sentences**

INVITE children to dictate a short message each morning. **WRITE** the sentences on the chalkboard, reciting sentence rules as you are writing. ("I start the sentence with a capital letter. I'm leaving spaces between words. I put a period at the end.") At some point **INTRODUCE** children to the "sentence rules" on page 28 in the handbook.

Favorite Part . . . . **Journals**

After reading a story to the children, **ASK** them to write the title and author on a page in their journal. **HAVE** them illustrate a favorite part and/or write about it. To encourage independence, **DEMONSTRATE** ways of spelling, using the tips on page 21 of the handbook. (Model and review these tips often.)

Some minilessons are extensions of the handbook. ···········▶

The Forms of Writing

Some minilessons relate directly to information and guidelines in the handbook material. ···········▶

Making a Plan . . . . **Clusters**

INTRODUCE the cluster on page 46 of the handbook. **READ** the story on page 47 and **EXPLAIN** how the cluster is a plan for the story. **DRAW** a blank cluster on the chalkboard. **WRITE** a central idea—a school assembly, field trip, or class project. **INVITE** children to fill the cluster. After finishing it, **USE** this cluster for discussing the central idea.

Getting Started Activities 9

More About
Minilessons . . .

Minilessons included with the teacher's chapter notes in the *Program Guide* are designed to introduce a concept, to review a basic skill, or to extend an idea introduced in the handbook.

Some minilessons are related to writing units.

Minilessons for Writing Stories About Me

Family Times . . . . **Writing Stories About Me**

READ or **TELL** a favorite story about families. **ASK** children what they do with their families to help, play, and share. **INVITE** them to tell about their families' favorite activities. **LIST** these on a chart to display in the classroom.

Something for You . . . . **Writing Stories About Me**

HELP the children **USE** their finished stories to make a keepsake poster or greeting card as a gift for their families.

A Happy-Time Plan . . . . **Writing Stories About Me**

To **MODEL** a plan for a specific story, **USE** the blackline master "Happy-Time Plan." **POINT OUT** the main idea, written in the center. Then **EXPLAIN** that answering the specific questions on the cluster will help them get ideas for their stories. (This is a good activity for small groups.)

Authors' Stories . . . . **Writing Stories About Me**

READ autobiographical stories like Patricia Polacco's *Thundercake* or Tomie dePaola's *The Art Lesson* to spark a discussion about ideas to use for story writing.

Minilessons for Word-Study Skills

Hunt and List . . . . **Consonant Blends**

DIVIDE the class into teams of four to six children. **RECALL** the definition of a blend (see handbook page 122). Then **GIVE** each team a long strip of paper. **INVITE** them to hunt for and list all the words they can find that begin with blends. (You may want to guide them to books and areas where words are readily available.) After hunting and listing, **MEET** to make a class list of blends.

Digraph Steps . . . . **Consonant Digraphs**

DRAW a large ladder or series of steps on the board with the digraphs "sh," "wh," "ch," and "th" on them. **HAVE** children take turns saying and writing words for the digraphs on each step.

Go fishing. . . . . **Short Vowels**

DRAW eight simple outlines of fish on the chalkboard. **WRITE** one short-vowel word on each fish. **ASK** volunteers to name the word on the fish, and then erase the whole thing with a "fishing pole," the eraser. At another time, this game may be played as a small-group activity. Children can use handbook page 124 as a starter.

New Words . . . . **Long Vowels**

WRITE these short-vowel words on the chalkboard:

    can cap cut Tim rod

HAVE children say the words and dictate a sentence using each of them. (Write the sentences on the chalkboard.) Next **ADD** a final "e" to each word. Then have students say the long-vowel words and dictate five more sentences. **DISCUSS** how the sound and the meaning completely change for these words, just by adding an "e."

Some minilessons are related to word-study skills.